CW00546270

TO MY DREC

BETH.

All MT LoE

ADAM
X

The Way of The Diva® is a registered trademark belonging to Adam Goodman-Smith.

© Adam Goodman-Smith, 2023.

The moral rights of the author have been asserted.

All rights reserved. No part of this book may be reproduced by any mechanical, photographic or electronic process or in the form of a phonographic recording; nor may it be stored in a retrieval system, transmitted or otherwise be copied for public or private use, other than for 'fair use' as brief quotations embodied in articles and reviews, without prior written permission of the author.

The information given in this book should not be treated as a substitute for professional medical advice; always consult a medical practitioner. Any use of information in this book is at the reader's discretion and risk. The author cannot be held responsible for any loss, claim or damage arising out of the use, or misuse, of the suggestions made, the failure to take medical advice or for any material on third-party websites.

THE WAY OF THE DIVA®

YOUR GUIDE TO A BOLDER, BRAVER
AND MORE CONFIDENT YOU

by Adam Goodman-Smith

FOLLOW THE WAY OF THE DIVA

thewayofthediva.com

It's hard being a diamond in a rhinestone world.
— Dolly Parton

BAREFOOT COACHING

Training as a coach with Barefoot Coaching changed my life in ways I could never have imagined.

To my Barefoot Coaching family, thank you for providing me with the inspiration and encouragement to make this book happen.

To Andy, thank you for seeing something in me all those years ago. Thank you for being my mentor and for speaking my name so generously in the right circles. I dread to think what my working life would be like had our paths never crossed. I remain eternally grateful and privileged that they did.

To Kim, thank you for changing my life, not once, but twice. Firstly, with your transformational teaching. And secondly, by encouraging me to be more of myself, from which The Way of The Diva was born. Without you, this book would have looked and sounded very different - if it had ever come to be.

I count myself lucky to work with such amazing people who are making a difference in the world.

Adam Goodman-Smith
Head of DIVAS
(**D**esign, **I**nspiration, **V**oice **A**nd **S**ocial Media)

THANK YOU

To Andy, Gracie, Ruby and all my wonderful family, thank you for your love, encouragement and support.

To a special someone (you know who you are), thank you for all you taught me. Thank you for the days spent watching Doris Day and Judy Garland movies. Most importantly, thank you for teaching me at the age of five how to enter and exit a car gracefully whilst protecting my modesty with an evening clutch bag. I hold you fully responsible for the diva I've become.

Adam x

THE WAY OF THE DIVA

INTRODUCTION

DEAR DIVA,

What drew you to pick up this book? Was it the catchy title? The colourful cover? Or was it something else? Something more profound? A quiet knowingness perhaps that you are, and have always been, more powerful than you could ever imagine. That you are worthy and deserving of everything this world has to offer. That all you have to do is have faith in yourself and you can live the kind of life you dream about. So, what's stopped you before? Fear of failure? Fear of success? Fear of being more of yourself, of speaking your mind and how that might change things? Regardless of the reason, my dear Diva, know that you've arrived at the right place at the right time. Stuff's about to get real, are you ready?

There's no such thing as an ordinary person or an ordinary life. You are one of 8 billion people on this planet, possibly in the entire universe. You are, by your very existence - extraordinary. I hope you realise how special you are. How important you are to this world. Because the world needs you, dear Diva. It needs you to embrace every bit of yourself - the light, the shade and everything in between. It needs you to believe in yourself and to speak your truth, whatever that may be. We haven't found ourselves by accident, you and I. You're here because you are meant to be. My instincts tell me that you are searching for something. Maybe it's more belief in yourself. Perhaps it's learning to stand up for yourself and to put an end to people taking advantage of you. Maybe you're looking for more confidence, happiness or a greater sense of meaning and purpose in your life. Perhaps you're just here for a good time - for the sass and the gags. Whatever the reason and whatever you're looking for - I'm here to help you find it.

This book has been almost a decade in the making. It takes the best of what I know about real life, human behaviour, personal development, psychology and coaching, and it marries it with everything I know about how to be a confident and self-assured diva. I hope that the result feels real, relevant and means you can start benefiting from the ideas, tools and techniques straight away.

I've spent my entire career in the business of people, from Retail to HR and from Training to Coaching. I've watched, I've observed and I've learnt. I've seen people at their very best and I've seen people at their worst. I've grown to know with some certainty that in the face of change, stress, strain and overwhelm, even the most capable and successful of people can lose sight of who they are and all that they bring to this world. Far too often, even the strongest, most resilient and capable people can, without too much effort, become their own worst enemies:

- They entertain the nagging little voice in their head that tells them they aren't good enough, that they aren't worthy and that if they try, they will fail.

- They become more concerned with what will happen if things go wrong, than if they went right.
- They compare their own story - their achievements, talents and possessions, to that of others, making up all sorts of stories that just aren't true. *She's two years younger than me and look at what she has that I haven't.*
- Whether they succeed or 'fail', they become obsessed with what other people might say about them - that they'd poke fun or be mean.
- They ruminate on conversations they've had and drive themselves mad attempting, and failing, to fill in the gaps. *What did they mean when they said that?*
- When they do well, they downplay their success. *Well, anybody could have done that; it doesn't make me special.*
- Both at work and home, they allow 'imposterism' to set in. *It was down to luck that I got here; at any moment they will find me out and I'll lose it all.*
- They place their own needs and desires at the bottom the priority list, insisting instead that other people's happiness is more important than their own.
- They become a passenger in their life, waiting for 'their turn', hoping that success will find its way to them when the time is right.

INTRODUCTION

This book calls bullshit on all of this and more. If you recognise any of what you've heard so far in your own behaviour, and you are ready to do something about it, then this book is written for you. If you are fortunate enough not to have to face some of the challenges I've described, then I ask that you take these tools and principles and use them to help those around you who, at times, can be their own worst enemies. Even better, gift them a copy of this book!

You see, our time here is finite, dear Diva - it's a brief flash in the pan, blink and it's gone. The universe had to wait 13.8 billion years for you to show up. Do yourself (and the universe) a favour and make that wait worthwhile. Get out there, be fabulous, strut your stuff, love yourself and love others. Make the most of your time here. Be the diva you are and have always been. Make shit happen. Do good out there and receive 'good' in return.

In the words of Mae West, a true Hollywood diva light-years ahead of her time...

You only live once, but if you do it right, once is enough.

Adam
X

THE WAY OF THE DIVA

Before we get started, the first thing I need you to do is to forget everything you know about the traditional 'Hollywood Diva'. Where the divas of the past were bitchy, unkind, demanding and looked down on people - the modern-day diva is altogether different. We do share some common traits, however, and those are about knowing our worth, standing in our power, believing in ourselves, being confident, assertive and making life happen *for us* rather than *to us*.

It may sound obvious, but it took me way too long to realise that one of the most beautiful things about this life is that we can be more than one thing.

We can be:

- Confident AND Humble.
- Boundaried AND Kind.
- Vulnerable AND Resilient.
- Modest AND Driven.
- Compassionate AND Steadfast.

As modern-day divas, we are role models for all that is good in the world. By embracing The Way of The Diva, without knowing it, we inspire those around us to stand in their power - possibly for the very first time.

Know also that a diva knows no bounds. We are every gender, age, shape, size and shade. Yes. I'm talking about you.

EGO: THE DIVA IN OVERDRIVE

Ego is the enemy of the diva. It's that little voice inside our head that tells us that we're the best thing since sliced bread and whilst confidence is great, and self-appreciation is an important part of what it means to be a diva, having too much ego can undermine all of our great diva work.

When a person's ego goes into overdrive, they risk becoming one of those divas from the past. They start to think that they're invincible; they believe that they're always right and that their way is the only way. They stop listening to what others have to say and start charging their way through life like a bull in a china shop. And, whilst they may think that they're impressing people with their confidence, they're actually pushing them away.

Here's the thing, having an oversized ego doesn't make you better than anyone else - it makes you a dick. So, if we want to be truly successful in life, we need to learn how to keep our ego in check. That means listening to others, being open to new ideas and admitting when we're wrong. Most of all, it means being humble and recognising that we are not perfect. Nobody is.

People who are truly strong lift others up. People who are truly powerful bring others together - Michelle Obama

The Way of The Diva is to balance the best of both worlds. To have self-worth, self-belief and confidence AND to embrace humility, compassion, kindness and curiosity. On a scale of 'selfish bitch' to 'doormat', it looks like this.

<-The Selfish Bitch ---- *The Diva* ---- The Doormat->

A NOTE ABOUT THE UNIVERSE

Throughout this book, I refer to the universe. What I'm referring to here is a sort of collective consciousness working in our favour. If you prefer, you can replace this term with one that better suits your own beliefs about the world - be it God, Mother Nature or your own unconscious. Work it until it works for you.

BLAGS, NOT 'BRAGS'

Live your life as though everything is rigged in your favour.

This is an important distinction to make, dear Diva. *Bragging*, excessively proud and boastful talk about one's achievements or possessions, isn't the same as *blagging*.

When it comes to blagging, there are many definitions and most, aren't terribly positive, 'to deceive', 'to trick' or 'to convince others for one's own personal gain.'

As with much in life, context and intention make all the difference. In the context of this book, the only person we are convincing of our worth, our abilities, our talents and our potential - is ourselves. And we do so with the intention of helping us to live a happier and more fulfilling life. A life in which modelling what it means to be a diva is, in itself, an act of service - to ourselves and others. Blagging in this sense, is not about deceit, ego, status or pride, but a technique for getting us out of our thoughts: *I can't, I'll never, I'm not*, and into the real world: *I can, I will, I am*. Bear this in mind as you read - context and intention are the sugar and spice of existence. They have the power to transform any dish, and in doing so, bring it to life.

HOW SHOULD I USE THIS BOOK?

We don't do rules, dear Diva; we make them. My advice is to pick it up and start anywhere. There might be a chapter that you like the sound of or that feels particularly relevant to your life right now. Don't wait - jump right in and start benefiting from the ideas and techniques straight away.

I didn't want to write a sequential book - the kind that said, 'Follow these ten steps in this order and you will change your life'. For this reason, the chapters are laid out in no particular order. Go wherever you are drawn to and if you come across something that resonates, don't be afraid to circle, underline, scribble or dog ear the pages - the margins are generous for this very reason. I'd love for you to keep coming back to this book whenever you need a burst of inspiration or when you need to be reminded of your brilliance.

TAKE IT OR LEAVE IT

There's a saying used often at Barefoot Coaching (my day job), 'Beware the person of one book'. It means to be open to multiple versions of the truth, to challenge any 'one way' of doing things and to be wary of anyone professing to have all the answers.

I do not profess to be an expert and I certainly don't always take my own advice. What I do know, however, is that when practised consistently - this stuff works, but by no means do you need to do it all. As you read, I encourage you to do two things:

1. Ask yourself: How could this help me in my life right now *and* how could I use it in a way that feels right for me?
2. Take what you like and leave the rest for some other time. Some parts will resonate more than others - that's OK. If you come back in a few weeks, it might well be that other parts take on more meaning.

Let us not take ourselves too seriously.
None of us has a monopoly on wisdom
- Queen Elizabeth II

—CONTENTS—

—CHAPTER ONE—

CONFIDENCE

A diva knows that those who shine from within don't need the spotlight.

CONFIDENCE IS A MYTH

There. I said it. Confidence does not exist as a thing in and of itself. Rather, it's a by-product of having your shit together in other areas of your life. It's no wonder then that it's frustrating to be told by your boss or your family and friends that you need to have more confidence or to 'just BE' more confident. Well, here's the news honey, it ain't that easy. For those of you who have been told this and were left scratching your head trying to figure out what was meant and how on earth you could flick a switch and suddenly wake up the next day as a more confident and self-assured person, hear me when I say - it's bullshit. You are not going mad; you are not crazy. If you've tried and haven't succeeded, you are not a failure - you just haven't landed on the right recipe...yet.

So, if confidence isn't a 'thing', what is it? Well, there's an analogy that I like to use to demonstrate this point and it's that of a cocktail - well this is The Way of The Diva, and we are divas after all.

Confidence is a drink served to taste. Each is different, that's the point.

THE CONFIDENCE COCKTAIL

STEP 1: Prepare your ingredients.

- Self-Awareness: Knowledge of who you are and what makes you unique.
- Values: The things that are important to you in how you live your life and how you are with others - the things that you stand for.
- Boundaries: What you will and won't tolerate from yourself and from others (the 'self' bit is important).
- Goals/Priorities: Knowing where you are heading in life and what you want for yourself.
- Assertiveness: Being able to stand up for yourself when required.
- Strengths: Awareness of what gives you energy and makes you feel good.
- Beliefs: Positive stories that you tell yourself about yourself.
- Self-Esteem: A quiet knowing that you are worthy and are loved.
- Self-Care: Investing time in yourself because you're worth it!
- Perspective: Being able to see the bigger picture, particularly when times get tough.
- Support From Others: Knowing that you can rely on the support and backing of those around you.
- And finally, a good splash of champagne; I'm just saying it helps.

STEP 2: Put it all into a shaker, add a good amount of ice and mix.

STEP 3: Serve, and this next bit is important, in a champagne saucer (a coupé), not a flute. Legend has it that the shape of this glass was modelled on Marie Antoinette's breast. So, I suppose it's 'tit's up' rather than 'bottoms'!

You might find it helpful to cast your eyes over those ingredients again, this time whilst asking yourself these questions:

- Which ingredients do you already have?
- Which could do with topping up?
- Which do you currently have less of?
- Which did you have in the past but have since lost somewhere along the way?

And finally, because we can't do it all.

- If you were to focus on getting your hands on one, maybe two, of these ingredients - which would they be? What difference would they make to you?

Throughout the book, I'll touch on every single one of these ingredients. For now, just enjoy the process of reading and trust that whatever you want will come. On the next few pages, I've included some quick, easy and hopefully fun techniques for topping up your confidence cocktail. If you like them, share them with a friend and enjoy them together.

Confidence isn't thinking that you are better than anyone. It's not having to compare yourself to anybody in the first place.

USE YOUR VOICE

Speaking your truth is a good place to start, dear Diva. Don't keep bottling up your thoughts and feelings - it's time to let it all out and let the world hear what you have to say. Too often, we shy away from speaking up because we're afraid of what others might think. It can be scary to put yourself out there and risk criticism or backlash. But guess what? That's how you grow. By facing your fears head-on and embracing your vulnerability, you'll start to build up a sense of self-worth and self-respect that can't be shaken. Let me tell you, there's no better feeling than letting your voice be heard and watching people sit up and listen to what you have to say. Whether it's in a meeting, with your friends or even just with yourself, speaking your truth is cathartic, it's empowering and what's more, the more you speak your truth, the more confident you become and the more you get to understand what your truth is.

Your voice is your gift to the world. Through your voice you are able to stand up for yourself, to stand up for others and bring about positive change in areas which you care about. Granted, it's not easy for one voice to change the world, but speaking your truth can change your world, dear Diva. You might be thinking, *Well, I don't know what I care about.* To that I say, you don't know what you care about - yet. If this sounds like you, take a look at the chapter titled 'Standing Up For Yourself'. It will help you get clearer on what you stand for and, equally as importantly, what you will not tolerate. Knowing what you stand for allows you to use your voice to speak your truth with meaning and purpose.

Nobody else is going to speak your truth for you. You're the only one who knows your thoughts and feelings, so it's up to you to share them with the world. The world needs your unique perspective and voice. Don't allow anyone else to silence you or make you feel like your voice doesn't matter. You are important and your words have value. So go ahead and speak your truth, dear Diva - you never know who might be listening and who you might inspire to do the same.

LOVE THE SKIN YOU'RE IN

Your body is gifted to you upon entering this world. Its role is to sustain your human form for as long as you are lucky enough to be around. You only get one - body, that is. For the last however many years you've been here, your body has carried you through every minute of every day. It's seen you through every challenge and difficulty, through every win and achievement, through the good times and the less good times. It's propped you up at every low point and it's danced with you at every high point. For those of you with small people, it's brought new life into this world. And yet, despite the important role it plays, all it asks for in return is that you give it fuel and whack on a bit of SPF every now and then.

You'd think that as we are one with our body, the relationship between us would be a delightfully happy one, one in which we skip gleefully together from one place to the next, grass between our toes and wind in our hair. But as I've experienced myself, that's not always the case. Despite being our closest friend, neighbour and loyal servant, the relationship between us can be fraught, to say the least. We can, at times, treat it in a way in which we'd never dream of treating somebody else, let alone someone who'd been by our side since day dot. For example, we might say all sorts of awful things to it. We might punish it by overdoing exercise or limiting its fuel intake. We might push and squeeze it into clothes that just aren't meant for it. We might rob it of the opportunity to bask in the sun or cool off in the breeze by covering it in layers and layers of dark clothing; you get where I'm going with this. Despite knowing that our body is part of us - we can treat it, and therefore ourselves, like dirt.

Treat yourself like somebody you are responsible for taking care of.

Self-disclosure time. I've had an unhappy relationship with my body, specifically my weight, since the age of 13. I've been just about every size and shape it's possible for one body to be. I've mistreated my body, I've hurt it, I've starved it, I've overfed it, I've over-exercised, over-indulged and 'over-everything'd'. I've made myself miserable. I've missed out on opportunities because of my perceived size (some potentially big ones too) and I've been miserable at times when I should have been at my happiest. Something changed for me as a direct result of writing this book. I found an acceptance in myself that I hadn't experienced before. After decades of body-bashing bullsh*t, here's where I've arrived:

It is possible to be heavier than I'd like and still...

- Be happy.
- Be healthy.
- Be fabulous.
- Do the things I want to.
- Visit the places I want to.
- Enjoy a day at the beach.
- Take that photo.
- Enjoy shopping for clothes.
- Enjoy putting outfits together.
- Wear bright colours.

- Stand out in a crowd.
- Let my personality shine.
- Not compare myself to anybody.
- Book that spa day.
- Have that massage.
- Take care of myself.
- Talk to myself kindly.
- Be a loud and proud diva.

If you recognise any of this in yourself, then I need you to hear this next bit loud and clear...

Your value is not measured in pounds or kilograms. Read that again.

I've spent way too long writing off experiences, places visited and things I'd achieved on account of being heavier. I told myself all sorts of nonsense. For example, *I'll have to come here again when I'm lighter so that I can take selfies.* Or, *What's the point in going if I can't put a picture on social media?* I dreaded going to events where I knew I'd see people who last saw me when I was lighter. I made life miserable for myself and for what gain? No gain. In fact, the opposite; I robbed myself of new experiences, of happiness, of opportunities and of meeting new people.

It's important to say that body image issues aren't just experienced by people who consider themselves heavier. I know lots of people who have been told by their GP that they are underweight and who experience the exact same issues I've described but for the opposite reason. For every one of us who is unhappy being heavier, there's somebody out there who is both lighter and utterly miserable. And, of course, people experience body issues for all sorts of reasons, not just size or shape.

> *Since I don't look like every other girl, it takes a while to be okay with that. To be different. But different is good – Serena Williams*

So, what can you do if, for whatever reason, you aren't feeling great about your appearance right now? Here are some things that I've found helpful.

- Recognise that 'healthy' isn't a size.
- Understand that your self-worth is not determined by your weight or shape.
- Know that you can have an amazing day even if you aren't comfortable with how you look.
- Understand that we aren't all supposed to look the same.
- Recognise that we are all unique and valuable in our own way.
- Notice and challenge any negative self-talk. Is it true? Is it helpful?
- Focus on the things you like about your body.

- Realise that your appearance tells the story of everybody who came before you.
- Stop comparing yourself to others - comparison is the thief of joy.
- Focus on what your body can do for you, rather than how you think it looks.
- Know that criticising your body won't change it - you're only hurting yourself.
- Surround yourself with body-positive influences.
- Unfollow social accounts that lead you to feel crap about yourself.
- Practise complimenting others on more than just their looks.
- Practise saying nice things to yourself about your body.
- Take small steps to accept yourself as you are and celebrate the wins.

For example:

1. Go out in public without covering up, e.g. lose the sweater, cardigan, coat, etc.
2. Experiment with new or different outfits.
3. Wear something a bit more fitted.
4. Wear your birthmarks, scars, tattoos and other markings with pride - they are part of what makes you who you are.
5. Wear your hair au naturel!
6. If one day you don't feel like putting on makeup, don't!

7. Ditch the dark colours for a day and wear something light or bright. People will see you regardless, so it's pointless trying to hide - you might as well have fun!
8. Say yes to an event or opportunity, even when every bit of you is saying no.
9. Whichever bit of your appearance you feel you need to hide - show it off and be proud of it. If you catch people looking, know that it's because you are inspiring them to do the same!

Here's my advice to you, and to myself. If any of what you've read is ringing true, then know this - life is too damn short to be getting in your own way like this. Don't waste a second longer telling yourself stories about what your appearance means you can or can't do. Go out there; chin up and celebrate every single bit of what makes you, you. Your body is the way in which you navigate this crazy world. Without it, there is no you - there is no diva. Wear your body like the most fabulous, priceless, one-of-a-kind outfit that it is. One day you will look back at pictures of yourself and wish that you had. This poem by Baz Luhrmann says it all.

Enjoy the power and beauty of your youth, oh, never mind.

You will not understand the power and beauty of your youth. Until they've faded, but trust me, in 20 years, you'll look back at photos of yourself and recall in a way you can't grasp now. How much possibility lay before you and how fabulous you really looked.

You are not as fat as you imagine.

Everybody's Free by Baz Luhrmann

I end with a technique gifted to me by Kim Morgan, CEO of Barefoot Coaching. It's a simple yet powerful way of seeing yourself through different eyes.

STEP 1:

Imagine that your 90-year-old self is standing at the opposite end of the room:

- What do you look like at 90?
- What's different about your appearance?

STEP 2:

- Walk towards this 90-year-old you, step into their shoes and look back at the younger you standing where you'd been.
- What did you think about how you looked back then?
- How much did you appreciate your beauty at the time?
- What words of advice or wisdom would you give to your younger self about your appearance?

STEP 3:

When you've had enough, return to your present-day self...and this next bit is really important.

Cut yourself some goddamn slack (my addition!).

Don't waste your life worrying about your body. This is your vessel. It's your house. It's where you live, there's no point in judging it.
– Emma Thompson

EVEN DIVAS WOBBLE

Yes, divas are self-assured, assertive and confident of their place in the world, but that still takes work and we are still human. The good news is that I've found the more you work on it, the easier it becomes. Confidence breeds confidence. It's also catching. People will notice the difference that this work makes to you. You will vibrate differently and they'll want a piece of that pie for themselves.

This type of work takes effort and requires consistent action. Here's an example to demonstrate.

OLD THOUGHT > OLD ACTION (OR NON-ACTION) > SAME OLD RESULT > REINFORCES SAME OLD BELIEF

NEW THOUGHT > NEW ACTION > NEW RESULT > LEADS TO NEW BELIEF

Example:

If I try x, it'll all go wrong > I don't try > I don't get what I want > Old thought reinforces old 'non-action', which reinforces old belief.

Alternatively:

I'm going to give it a go > I give it a go and the world doesn't end > *Hmm, maybe I can do this after all* > New thought > I give it a go next time and it goes a bit better > *I think there's a chance I could actually make this work* > New thought challenges old thought, which challenges old belief, and so on.

When it comes to changing the way you think and therefore the way that you behave, know this:

- Small, even minute changes add up.
- Consistency and patience are key.

You can't choose the thoughts that enter your head. But you can choose the ones you tell to f*ck off.

HOW YOU TALK TO YOURSELF MATTERS

Is there any more to say here, dear Diva? Let me break it down for you. You are the most influential person in your life. What you think, say and do determines your view on not just what you are capable of doing, but at a fundamental level, what you believe you are worthy of doing.

Think of that gorgeous brain of yours as a supercomputer. If you put good stuff in, you get good stuff out. If you put shit in, you get shit out.

It's as simple as that. Make friends with yourself, get alongside yourself and start working with yourself, rather than against. Together, you can achieve great things, incredible things, but only if you stop:

- Telling yourself that you aren't good/worthy enough.
- Telling yourself that other people matter more than you do.
- People pleasing and putting other people's needs and priorities above your own.
- Apologising for things that don't require an apology.
- Comparing yourself to others.
- Hiding what you think and what you're capable of.

- Doubting yourself and your abilities.
- Fearing failure.
- Finding reasons and excuses for putting off what you really want and who you want to be.
- Putting up with shitty people and shitty situations.

Here's the nub of it. If someone tells you something often enough, you begin to think it's true. The same goes for how you choose to talk to yourself.

If you were to go a little bit easier on yourself today, to give yourself a break, to be a little bit nicer to yourself - what would you say?

READ YOUR FAN MAIL

As important as it is for a diva to be their own number one fan, sometimes it's nice to hear from others. Now listen up, if you are going to do this then there is one rule and one rule only - you have to believe what they tell you. There's no point opening your fan mail, reading all those lovely words and then brushing it off with, *Of course they'd say that - they're my friend.* Or, *Yeah, it's nice, but it's not true.* You have no business saying what other people do or do not believe; that's their business. If you're going to invite it, accept it graciously, absorb it, feel its warmth and let it nourish you. Otherwise, don't bother.

Here's how it goes. Ask five people whom you respect and trust the following questions. Have them text or email you their answers so that you can keep them to look back on. In return, you might invite them to do the same.

- What one word or phrase describes me best?
- What are my best qualities?
- What are my greatest strengths?
- What do you think is my greatest achievement?
- What one thing could I change for my own benefit?

Credit: Barefoot Coaching

BUILD YOUR BAD BITCH BOARD

What on earth is a 'Bad Bitch Board'? I hear you ask. Well, you're about to find out. Do you remember how at school you'd keep all your certificates and awards in a folder? A sort of evidence log of everything you'd achieved academically, plus a few nice commendations from friendly dinner ladies. The idea was that you'd take this folder along to job interviews because whoever was interviewing you would like to, no, make that *expect* to see it. I mean they never did ask to see it, well in my case anyway. Despite it not being as widely read as we'd been led to believe, it did have value. I was going through the contents of my first flat earlier this year, contents that had been sitting in my Mum's loft for twenty-plus years. I came across said folder, a sort of reddish-brown faux leather thing with gold lettering. As I opened it, despite its sparsity, something came over me. As well as early 90's nostalgia, there was a sense of pride and achievement as I read the comments and reports - all the very best bits of my academic achievement recorded in one place for me to look back on and smile. Consider your 'Bad Bitch Board' the modern equivalent, a place for you to keep note of all the wonderful things that make you who you are. Your achievements, the things that are important to you in life, nice things that people have said about you, etc. A place to come back to as often as you need, whenever you require a little boost or pick me up. There are no rules as to how you create it. Some people buy themselves a pinboard and create a physical collage. Others might use a notepad or perhaps even keep a log online, a sort of Pinterest type thing. Whatever works for you. My only advice is to keep it somewhere where you can easily access it at the point of need. As I said, that point of need might be when you've had a bad day and you need a boost or it might be when you are preparing for a job interview, or when you need to write something about yourself. The job interview point is a good one because if you've ever been asked the question, *So, tell us about yourself?* Or perhaps something a bit more abstract like, *If you were a bird, what sort of bird would you be and why?* And you've just sat there and gone blank, well having created your 'BBB', you'd have something to go off of - perhaps not the bird thing, but it'd at least give you somewhere to start.

Here are some examples of the things you could include on your BBB:

- Your strengths. These are the things that you are good at and enjoy doing.
- Your values. These are the things that are important to you in life.
- Things that make you happy.
- Things that drain your energy.
- What you are like when you are feeling great.
- Your skills and talents.
- Things that you want to achieve.
- The things that make you unique.
- Your successes / achievements to date.
- Things that you have overcome.
- Nice things that people have said about you.
- Things that you'd like people to be saying about you when you aren't there.

It might feel self-indulgent, and to that I say - and? In a world where there is so much negativity all around us, why not create a place you can go to when you need to remind yourself of just how bloomin' amazing you are, of all the good that's in you and how without a shadow of a doubt - you've got this, boo. Give it a go. You might just be surprised at the difference it makes.

It's time to remember who the hell you are.

CONFIDENCE TIMELINE

It's likely that your relationship with confidence has changed over time. Just today, I was talking to somebody about how only eight or so years ago, I'd have driven myself to the airport and flown to Paris alone to meet my husband for the weekend - something I wouldn't do nowadays. So what's changed? Probably not a whole lot, except that my life is different now; it's not the kind of thing I'd do on a whim anymore. I don't like driving on the motorway, I'd find getting through the airport stressful, but what it really comes down to is that I've fallen out of the habit. I haven't done that sort of thing for such a long time now.

This conversation got me thinking about the idea of a confidence timeline. A timeline where we can track points in our past where we did feel confident and could recount what we did and how it made us feel. The idea is that by labelling it, we can try to bring some of that confidence back into our lives right now.

Here's how it works:

1. Draw a line that represents a period of time that makes sense to you - it could be the last month, year or decade.
2. Think about points within that timeline where you felt confident and plot them.

3. For each point, reflect on the following:
   - What were you doing?
   - Who were you with?
   - Specifically, what was it about the situation that made you feel confident?

Once complete, step back and observe any patterns or themes which stand out to you.

What actions could you take to bring more of that confidence into your life right now? That might include the things you were doing or the qualities of the people you were with.

Pay attention to who you are with when you feel at your best.

GET STRETCHING

No, I'm not talking about yoga or Pilates - this is more about stretching your mindset and stepping outside of your comfort zone to achieve the things that you want. There's a saying...

If you always do what you've always done, you will always get what you've always got.

It makes sense then, that if you want to achieve a different result, you need to think and behave in a different way. A way that in the beginning, might feel scary.

In my experience, the thing that holds most people back from doing the things they desire, is themselves. It's their frame of mind rather than any distinct lack of talent, knowledge or skill. We are, at times, our own worst enemies. But why?

It's been proven that fear presents itself physiologically in almost the exact same way as excitement. When you feel frightened, your brain sends messages to your body to increase both your breathing and heart rate. Your ears prick up and your hearing becomes sharper. Your pupils dilate, your muscles tense as you become primed for action and you might get butterflies in your stomach as blood is diverted away from your digestive system. When you feel excited, the exact same thing happens. The only thing that differentiates the two is how you interpret the situation. Is this a good or bad place? Am I safe or in danger? Should I stay or run? It's fair to say then, that when you feel fear, it's almost always down to your thoughts about the situation rather than the situation itself. Of course, some of that will be justified. For example, if the building is on fire, you can bet your bottom dollar that I'll be the first one out. But most of the time it won't be. For example, if you know that in order to get the promotion you want, you will need to go and present to the board and the idea of that makes you feel physically sick, first, I can empathise. Second, know that the fear you are feeling is no longer justified. The chances of you not making it out of that presentation alive are slim to none, but at the time, it can feel like life and death.

Our sense of danger and our innate response to it, both psychological and physiological, was formed in the early days of humankind. Back then its job was to protect us from threats and predators, to keep us alive at all costs in order to reproduce and propagate the human race. It's an unhelpful hang-up that served us hundreds of thousands of years ago, but is much less helpful now.

Here's where it gets interesting. With awareness comes choice. By tapping into what you are feeling in any given moment and asking yourself questions such as, What's going on here? What's making me feel this way? How helpful are these thoughts and feelings? You can make a conscious choice, in that moment, to take action regardless. To feel the fear and do it anyway. And the same is true as earlier, confidence breeds confidence. The more you step out of your comfort zone and not only survive but thrive, the more your comfort zone will expand and those things that scared the tits off you before, become commonplace in your life. How chuffing fabulous is that?

Being a diva is about putting yourself out there, playing the field and making things happen for yourself. Sitting and waiting for things to fall into your lap, waiting for people to reach out and find you, trusting that someone will pick up the phone and offer you your dream job, won't happen unless you take some sort of action.

Don't wait for your boat to come in. Row out and meet it.

If any of this is resonating with you, then take some time to think about your comfort zone:

- What nice moments have you had in your comfort zone?
- What fun times have you had when you stepped outside of your comfort zone?
- How could you stretch your comfort zone just a little bit more? Think about small steps, repeated.
- If you did, what would become possible that doesn't seem possible right now?

You owe it to yourself to at least try.

Most of the time if we are blocked in an area of our life - it's because we feel safer that way.
- Julia Cameron

YOUR COCKTAIL PARTY PITCH

This is my take on the old 'elevator pitch'. Those things move far too quickly nowadays to accommodate small talk. Before you know it, you're up 70 floors of the Shard before you can even say 'Cristal'. No, I much prefer a nice, gentle cocktail party introduction instead.

Picture it. You're dressed up and looking good. You have your glass of fizz and perhaps you've just taken a delicious looking microscopic canapé which goes down in one bite - which is good because you see someone heading your way. They make eye contact from across the room. You smile and brush away the rough puff stuck to your lippy. They seem important, expensive and connected. They look you in the eye and say, *Hello, I don't think we've met before. What is that you do?'*

And you reply with...

That was the bit where you were supposed to say something.

There's a saying I like by the infamous drag queen RuPaul...

If you stay ready, you ain't gotta get ready.

On a serious note, what would you say? It doesn't have to be knock 'em out of their heels amazing. But it does need to represent who you are and what you do. The delivery of course, is as important as the words you use. Here are some tips:

- Keep it short and snappy. *I'm Adam, I'm a writer and a coach and I help people live happier by being a bit more diva.* Bang. There. Done.
- Own it. Practise it in the mirror until it sounds like you believe what you are saying.
- Be clear about what you do. Don't just say, *I work in education.* Say, *I teach science to secondary school kids.*
- Don't overwhelm people with information. Give the headlines, get them interested and then leave them wanting more.
- Try and keep it light, even if your occupation isn't. If you dig graves for a living, then that's the time to keep it vague - actually, what kind of cocktail party is this?
- Don't use jargon. Use plain, simple language that your granny would understand. Nobody wants to have to think too much at a party, da-ling.
- Give people an opportunity to respond and then ask them about themselves.
- Have good eye contact, but don't stare.
- Keep the fidgeting and foot shuffling to a minimum.

Every room needs a focal point, dear Diva. Why not let it be you?

Allow people to be drawn to you, to be intrigued by you and to want to find out more about you. When they talk to you, make them feel like they are the only person in the room. Leave them feeling better about themselves than before they met you. Spread love, joy and positivity. Radiate what it means to be a diva.

OWN THE ROOM

This may surprise you, but for me, owning the room isn't about being the centre of attention or being the loudest or the most flamboyant. It's more a way of thinking and believing than of being. As with everything in life, you have a choice. You can choose to believe that you were lucky to get onto the guest list, that you're there to fill a seat, that you were the last choice or that nobody will be interested in what you have to say - and the whole thing, be it a meeting or a social event, will be an absolute 'disaaster, darling'. Or, you can follow The Way of The Diva. This approach is about believing:

- You're there because the host wanted you there.
- You're worthy, deserving and more than capable of holding your own amongst the other guests.
- You are an equal to the others in the room. Nobody is above or below another.
- The event and the other guests will be all the better off because you're there.
- You may make valuable connections that will benefit you at some point in the future.

- It is your duty as a diva to leave those you meet feeling noticed, appreciated and feeling better about themselves than they would had you never met. To be clear, this isn't about ego. It's about spreading kindness, love and compassion.

Your smile is your logo, your personality is your business card, and the way you make others feel is your trademark - Jay Danzie

Here are some tips to help you master the art of owning the room:

1. **Wear something that makes you feel good.** Dress in a way that makes you feel good - because when you feel good it shows, and you make other people feel good about being around you. Adding a pop of colour or a statement accessory will help you to get noticed and stand out in a crowd. This makes it easier when people are trying to find you to introduce you to somebody. The late Queen Elizabeth II made it her business to wear bright colours because it made her easy to spot in a crowd. She's quoted as saying, '*I have to be seen to be believed*', and that's stuck with me.

2. **Make good eye contact.** When you're speaking with someone, make sure that you maintain eye contact. It shows that you're engaged and interested in what they have to say. It also helps to build a connection with the person you're speaking to and lets them know that they've been seen. When you're addressing a group, try to meet the gaze of as many people in the room as possible. This will make them feel seen and included.

3. **Use open and relaxed body language.** Your body language speaks volumes about your confidence and credibility. Stand tall, maintain an open posture and try to relax. Relaxing is the key point here, because who are you trying to impress? Nobody. The only review that counts is the one you write yourself. You have nothing to prove to anybody, so act like it.

4. **Take your time, pause and remember to breathe**. When you're speaking to a group, yes, it's important to project your voice clearly and confidently, but it's even more important to take your time. To speak slowly and clearly, and to use pauses to emphasise important points. Your voice is your gift, dear Diva. Allow the audience to bathe in that gift and enjoy every moment of it. Give the fans what they want. On a practical note, avoid filler words like 'um' or

'like', as these break your flow and dumb down your vibe. Try recording yourself and then see how many times you use filler worlds. Instead, add in a brief pause and give yourself time to think about what you are going to say next.

5. **Be prepared.** Preparation is key if you're going to own the room. Whether you're giving a presentation or attending a social event, make sure that you've done your homework, that you're well-informed and have a clear understanding of what you want to achieve. This will help you to speak confidently and get your message across - it will also help you get noticed by the right people! If you can't swap numbers with the people you'd like to, try and get hold of the attendance list from the organisers. Sometimes a cheeky email or a phone call is all that's standing in the way of you fulfilling your dreams.

6. **Pay attention.** Owning the room isn't just about speaking confidently. It's also about listening actively. Make sure that you're paying attention to what others are saying and try to respond appropriately. This will help you to build rapport and 'vibe' with those around you. Who knows, if you do the job right, you may just have found the newest member of your entourage! More on that later.

COMMUNICATE LIKE THE DIVA YOU ARE

By this, I don't mean boss people around and demand that your grande latte-chino is extra hot. I mean speak and write from a place of assertiveness and self-assurance. A place that is clear and kind and communicates your own needs in a way that doesn't belittle yourself or others. I receive far too many emails that begin with, *I'm sorry to bother you.* Sorry? What on earth are you sorry for? Don't apologise for taking up space. If this sounds familiar to you, then stop. Quit it. Over-apologising for things that don't require an apology, let alone an over-apology, is doing nothing more than pissing off the recipient (perhaps I've touched my own nerve here, admittedly) and sending a clear and simple message to yourself that you don't matter as much as the next person. Now why would you do a thing like that? As with all things, practise makes perfect:

1. Start by being more conscious of the words you use, how you use them and whom you use them with. See if you notice any patterns.
2. Try swapping out some of the phrases you usually use on autopilot and see how it feels. Examples to follow.
3. Keep going until you find the sweet spot. It still needs to sound like something that you would naturally say.
4. Notice the difference in how you feel and also to the results you get.

Instead of:	Try:
Sorry I'm late	Thanks for waiting for me
Sorry for bothering you	Thanks for your time
Sorry for getting emotional	Thanks for letting me have a moment
Sorry I messed up	Thanks for spotting that
Sorry I can't make it	Thanks for the invite, however
Sorry for the delay	Thanks for bearing with me
Would it be OK if / would it be possible to / could you possibly...	What I need from you is...can we talk about how we make that happen?
I'm flexible, what works best for you?	Could you do...?
No worries / No problem	Happy to help
I hope that makes sense...	Let me know if you have any questions

Treat yourself with the same respect you offer to others and quit talking down to yourself.

Never apologise for:

- Taking up space. For living and breathing!
- Asking for what it is you need.
- Asking questions.
- Not being able to give others what they 'expect' from you.
- Your goddamn feelings.
- Not being 'perfect'.
- Not replying to messages and emails immediately.
- Making choices that are in your own best interest.
- Setting and maintaining healthy boundaries.
- Taking a break.
- Letting go of dead wood (cutting out negative people from your life).
- Prioritising your health and wellbeing.
- Outgrowing people or places.
- Doing what makes you happy.

Stop apologising for anything that doesn't warrant an apology – that includes apologising to people who bump into YOU!

DAILY AFFIRMATION

What better way to start the day than with some confidence-boosting self-talk. Here's a morning affirmation by actor and author Jennifer Lewis, which is a sure-fire way to get your day off to a great start. Jennifer says...

I brush my teeth.

I spit it out.

I look in the mirror.

I go ooh, ooh (dabs sides of mouth).

And then I lean forward, I pause, and I say these words...

PRETTY BITCH!

YOUR CONFIDENCE ANTHEM

Music is emotive. It has the power to transport us back in time and make us feel a certain way. Think about some of your favourite songs. I bet you can remember the first time you heard them, who you were with, what you were doing and what that time in your life meant to you. You might have songs that remind you of being a kid, e.g. nursery rhymes or TV theme tunes. Songs that remind you of your teenage years and all the wonderful, and perhaps naughty, things that you got up to. Songs that were playing when you met your partner, or that were played at your wedding. Songs that remind you of when your kids were small or songs that remind you of rocking out at your best friend's wedding. Music is powerful, and we can use that power to remind us of who we are, what we've achieved, how far we've come and what we've come through. When we feel down, when we've had a tough day or when we just need a pick me up, the right music can make all the difference. Whether you're taking to the stage at the start of your sell-out one-person show, are entering the boxing ring, are getting ready for a night out or you're plucking up enough courage to brave the school run - the anthem that's playing sets the scene for the show. It doesn't matter what it is, how long or short, how well-known or obscure the artist is, whether it contains meaningful words or rousing music. What matters is that it leaves you feeling a certain way. Ideally a way that has you going, *Yeah, come on, I've got this - give me your best shot.*

- If you had to choose a confidence anthem, what would it be?
- What's special about it to you?
- How does it make you feel when you listen to it?

You are, and have always been, 'That bitch'.

LEARN TO TRUST YOUR INSTINCTS

Your intuition is a gift, dear Diva. You might not have used it much, or you might have gotten used to ignoring it. Either way, it's there guiding and assisting you. Trusting your intuition, working with it rather than against it, can help build confidence in your ability to make good decisions that model who you are and what you believe in. Have you ever ignored your gut instinct and then regretted it? I know that I have.

Some say that our intuition is a kind of sixth sense, a way that the universe speaks to us through:

- Feelings: I feel uneasy around this person; they're giving me bad vibes, best to stay away.
- Thoughts: I need to call Adam because something is telling me he needs me.
- Physical sensations: The urge to cross the street just before a drunk driver mounts the curb.

Some argue that intuition is less of a superpower and more a natural ability that our brains have of processing the world around us at a much faster rate than the conscious mind can comprehend. Taking in millions, if not billions, of data points through our senses at any one point and processing them in such a way that leaves us thinking, *There's no way I could have known that!*

By noticing and acting on your intuition, you can start to make better decisions. Decisions that put your needs and goals up front and centre and, equally as important, you can stay clear of people who don't have your happiness high up on their agenda.

Tips for developing your intuition:

- When faced with a decision, as well as considering the facts, check in with what your instincts are telling you. How does the decision feel? Easy/right? Or is there something else? Something niggling.
- Ask yourself often, *What is my gut saying?* Listen for a reply. Then act on it and see how things work out differently for you.
- Stop. Hooold Up. Wait a Minute. Take a few minutes to check in with yourself and meditate on the situation. Find a quiet place where you won't be disturbed. Sit quietly, clear your mind, focus your attention on your breathing and then notice what you notice. What thoughts come to the forefront? Which come and go easily, and which are a bit harder to shake off? These are the ones to pay attention to.
- Pay attention to your dreams. Your dreams are a way in which your subconscious communicates. Notice the kind of dreams you're having. What helpful meaning can you draw from them?

- Act on your intuition. The more you notice the messages you're receiving and the more action you take in support of them, the more messages you will receive. It's a bit like listening out for the knock on the door. If you aren't listening out for it, if you're drowning out the silence with 'Saturday Night' by Wigfield playing at full blast, you aren't going to hear the knock. Turn down the volume in your head and give the knock a chance to get heard.

Trust your instincts. Intuition does not lie.
– Oprah Winfrey

JUST DO YOU

It's time to stop giving a shit about what other people think of you. Seriously, you don't have time for that nonsense. We only get one go, dear Diva. Don't spend yours trying to be anything other than who you are. You don't need anyone else's approval to live your best diva life. Let's face it, people are always going to have an opinion. They'll judge your clothes, your hair, your job, how you spend your time, your taste in music, your life choices and everything in between. But guess what? It's none of their business. You do you and let them do them. Sure, it's natural to want to be liked and accepted. But that doesn't mean you have to change who you are or what you believe in to fit someone else's idea of perfect. That's a recipe for disaster and a sure-fire way to lose yourself in the process. Embrace your quirks, your flaws, your passions and your dreams. Own them, love them and live your life on your terms. Because at the end of the day, the only opinion that truly matters is your own.

Why would you put your self-esteem in the hands of complete strangers?
– Helena Bonham Carter

- How could you be a bit more of yourself today?
- What would you do? What would you say?
- What activities and opportunities would you say yes to? And which would you tell to 'you know what'?

See the chapter titled 'Knowing Yourself' to assist you in 'doing you'.

CHAPTER TWO

KNOWING YOURSELF

A diva knows that they are totally unique - just like everyone else.

BE THE STAR THAT YOU ARE

Before you were in this life, you danced among the stars. You were part of the cosmos. Today, your human body is made up of carbon, therefore you are made up of the particles of former stars. You are a star in its next form.
– Kyle Gray

Take a moment, dear Diva, and sit with that thought for a moment. Do you have any idea how special you are? What a miracle it is that you are here on this rock reading this? It is a miracle - you, are a miracle. You are one of only eight billion people, on one planet, orbiting one star, amongst four billion stars, in one galaxy, amongst two trillion galaxies - and yet, as far as we know, it's just us. We are alone on what is possibly the only island of meaning. That's pretty awesome, right? And that means you are too.

Yet, so often, particularly under the weight of stress, strain, change and uncertainty, we can lose sight of just how special we are and how, despite being so alike, we are all so gloriously different, unique - precious. We know how society treats one-of-a-kind, precious items; they are treasured, worshipped and adored. The same, dear Diva, should be said of you.

Sadly, many people will go about their lives unaware of just how remarkable they are. Paying little attention to what makes them who they are, what drives their behaviour, what makes them unique: their qualities, passions, strengths and their higher purpose here on this Earth. So much can be gained from discovering more about ourselves. Not only does our life start to make sense, in that we begin to connect the dots between our thoughts, our behaviours, our actions and our results - but that knowledge becomes invaluable in determining where we go next.

Awareness = Choice.

Once we understand who we are and why we do what we do, we can make informed choices about whether we carry on doing what we've been doing and getting what we've been getting, or whether we want something different for ourselves. This insight is invaluable when it comes to directing our gaze and our focus in the direction of our desires.

Until you make the unconscious conscious, it will rule your life and you will call it fate.
- Carl Jung

Regardless of whether you buy into this or not, believe me when I say that you owe it to yourself to discover, or perhaps even rediscover, the star that you are.

LIGHTS, CAMERA, ACTION!

The scene is set, dear Diva. The audience of your one-person show awaits your opening monologue...

Who are you?

If that made you uncomfortable - good. That's a sign that you've come to the right place.

In theatre, sets change. People come and go. There are unexpected twists and turns. We laugh one minute and cry the next. The same can be said of life. These experiences can be formative. They can shape and re-shape us. Typically, the things that are important to us, the things we stand for, remain steady. But who we are, what drives us and how we show up in the world, can change.

You aren't who you were yesterday. And you aren't who you will become tomorrow.

With that in mind, I suppose my opening question should have been...

Who are you, today?

All the world's a stage and most of us are dreadfully under-rehearsed - Jennifer Coolidge

IT'S ALL ABOUT THE JOURNEY

The journey to self-discovery is, in my experience, one in which the destination is always just slightly out of reach. When you're heading down that road, your foot is on the gas and you are racing towards the beaming citadel on the horizon, you come over the final hill and...more road. To focus on the destination is to miss the point. We never stop learning about ourselves, which I suppose is what makes it so thrilling, a bit like a really good play - you never know what twists and turns lay ahead. My advice, therefore, is...

Focus on the process, not the product.

When you succumb to the notion that we are all merely works in progress, each of us just living moment to moment, doing the best we can with what we have, something happens. A weight is lifted and you can begin to enjoy the process, play with it, have fun with it and see where it leads you.

BEING YOURSELF

Knowing yourself can be made more challenging if you've spent your life pretending to be somebody you aren't. Your true self, your real preferences and desires may have been suppressed in favour of a perceivably more favourable, more acceptable façade. There are all sorts of reasons why this might have happened. It might have felt safer that way; you may have felt you needed to be a certain way for your job or perhaps to appease somebody else. Over time, this misalignment between *who* you are and *how* you are can be troublesome, to say the least. Like a square peg in a round whole, you don't fit. Your façade doesn't fit because you know it's an act and your true self doesn't fit because you feel as though you can't be who you really are. Psychologists describe this as Cognitive Dissonance and the long-term effects on a person's mental and physical well-being can be significant.

It might be that you've spent so long attempting to fit in that you've actually forgotten who you are. Or, as in my case, your sense of self has evolved and the environment you're in is no longer conducive to the version of you that is emerging.

If you don't know who you truly are, you'll never know what you really want.
– Roy T. Bennett

WHO ARE YOU WHEN NOBODY IS LOOKING?

I'd worked in the world of personal development and coaching for over a decade before I came across this very question in a pack of Barefoot Coaching's Coaching Cards for Everyday. When I think back to that time in my life, I see that moment as a turning point.

Up until that point, I was having a reasonably successful career. I had a nice house, I was happily married - everything was going well. But. I knew that something wasn't right. I was restless in my career; I knew that I wanted to do something different and that the 9-5 corporate gig just wasn't for me anymore. I also knew that I was capable of more; I just didn't know what. This question gave me the permission I didn't know I needed to think about who I was becoming, beneath the version of myself that showed up to my desk job each day, most of the time late. If you work for a big business and you do a decent job, opportunities and roles come along and your career becomes something that sort of happens to you. A project over here leads to a role over there. That's what happened to me. In a way, I'd spent 16 years sleepwalking my way into role after role, looking upon the title, the grade and the salary as my measures of success, whilst the size of the business and my long service offered me a degree of safety and security. Asking myself who I was when nobody was looking, was a wake-up call. An opportunity to dig deep and face the facts...what I was doing just wasn't me anymore.

So, now I offer you the same opportunity that was afforded to me.

Who are you when nobody is looking?

- What do you look like?
- What's your style? What clothes do you wear? Feeling that I had to dress in a certain way became a really big deal for me. Getting dressed in the morning actually made me cross. I'd look at all the gorgeous colours and slogan sweatshirts, funky trainers and jewellery just hanging there, whilst I reached for a grey/blue shirt and tie. Gosh, I'm getting flashbacks.
- What do you sound like? What do you say?
- How do you talk to yourself? Kindly?
- What activities/hobbies do you enjoy?
- What music do you listen to?
- What's your favourite TV show?
- What sort of work do you enjoy doing?
- What makes you happy?

Now pause and ask yourself, to what degree are you like this person now? If the answer is 'a lot', then good for you. You're living your truth and that's something special, something that in my experience few can say. If your answer is anything but 'a lot', then you, dear Diva, have some work to do.

Find out who you are - and do it on purpose.
- Dolly Parton

LIGHT AND SHADE

Awareness can also be gained by thinking about how you are during the best of times - when you're feeling absolutely shit hot, you're firing on all cylinders and smashing your way through life. As well as at the worst of times - when you are just about getting by, you are angry or upset, you are feeling defeated, you are running around like a headless chicken because you have so much to do and don't know where to start, or you retreat inward through overwhelm or fear.

What your friends and loved ones experience of you in these two states is important. Their insight can prove invaluable. Sometimes you are just too close to see what's going on for yourself, so ask some of them how they experience you in these two states.

Here's some food for thought.

When you feel at your absolute best, when everything is going your way and you are doing your best work:

- How do you behave?
- What does it feel like to be you?
- What are you able to achieve?
- What are you like to be around?

Now, let's flip it. When you feel like you are just about getting by, doing your best just to survive:

- How do you behave?
- What does it feel like to be you?
- What are the knock-on effects?
- What are you like to be around?

TRIGGERS AND SWITCHES

Remember earlier when I said that Awareness = Choice? Here is where it becomes relevant.

- What causes you to go from being at your best to just getting by? This could be anything from behaviours that really annoy you (your own or other people's), tasks/jobs, the amount of work you have on, things that people might say, unhelpful things that you might tell yourself, feeling scared, feeling like certain values are being trampled on like fairness, honesty, integrity etc. Anything at all that causes you to wobble.
- What are the early warning signs? How do you know it's coming?

And when you are in that place of just getting by:

- What lifts you out of it? What steadies the ship and brings you back up for air? This could be stepping out of the situation and taking five minutes to yourself, reminding yourself that you don't need to do it all alone, going for a walk, eating healthy and nourishing foods, repeating a positive mantra or it might be just sitting with it until it passes and trying not to be a dick to anybody in the meantime.

- Who do you turn to? What do they do that helps bring you back down to earth?

Whatever tips you over the edge and whichever strategies you use to get yourself back on track, know that this is all helpful data and insight about who you are, how you operate and what's important to you.

Your triggers are your teachers. Whatever triggers you reveals a part of you that still needs to be healed.

With this data comes awareness. With awareness comes choice. As a diva, you understand your unique set of pulleys and switches, the things that help you be and stay at your best, and equally, the things that trigger the heck out of you. This means that you can make informed choices about how to be at any given moment. Take notice of your early warning signs, dear Diva, and act in your own best interest, not only to protect yourself, but also the people around you. As divas, we are responsible and accountable for our actions and non-actions. We own our behaviour, especially when we mess up. We are only human after all.

OWN YOUR SHIT, OR IT WILL OWN YOU

I often say that other people's behaviour, more often than not, has absolutely nothing to do with the recipient and absolutely everything to do with the other person. It's pants, I get that and people do need to be more accountable for their behaviours and actions, especially if they cause harm. The unfortunate reality is that most of the time, this projection is subconscious - meaning the projector doesn't:

a.   Know that they are doing it.
b.   Understand why they are doing it.

Projection is a defence mechanism for dealing with all sorts of uncomfortable and potentially painful emotions. According to Sigmund Freud, the 'godfather of modern psychology', we project these emotions onto other people so that they become the carriers of our own perceived flaws, not us - essentially, *you're the problem, not me.*

Here are some examples:

- The person who bullies someone for being gay, who deep down has unanswered questions about their own sexuality.
- The person who has been unfaithful to their partner and then accuses their partner of cheating on them.
- The person who has a compulsion to steal

and guards their belongings for fear of others stealing from them.

- The adult who calls people fat or ugly who was bullied for their appearance in school.
- The 'realist' who likes to squash other people's goals and dreams because they themselves fear failure.

And so on. Because projection is subconscious, it's hard to know whether we are projecting onto others or not. One way to explore how this might be presenting in your own life is to think about people whom you either dislike or can become easily jealous of:

- What is it about them that you dislike?
- If you were to attribute that characteristic or behaviour to yourself, what connection could you make?
- What's really going on here? How might that thing you dislike about them be a projection from you, onto them?

Here's an example:

I used to sit opposite somebody whom I didn't trust. I'd even go as far as to say I didn't like them. If I was to attribute what I disliked about this person to myself, I'd say that I could see how people could, at times, experience the same sarcastic and slightly bitchy vibe that I got from them, in their interactions with me - of course I hope that wasn't the case! What I think was really going on, is that I was worried that this person might talk about me in the same way that I talked about them! Jeez, we teach what we need to learn, right?

Everything that irritates us about others can lead us to an understanding of ourselves.
- Carl Jung

PARENT, ADULT OR CHILD?

Sticking with the theme of relationships for a moment, the Parent-Adult-Child model can help us understand the different roles we play in our relationships. It was developed by psychiatrist Eric Berne in the 1950s and is based on the idea that we all have three ego states: Parent, Adult and Child. Each ego state influences our behaviour and therefore how we communicate:

Parent: This is where we take care of others. This ego state is made up of learned behaviours, beliefs and habits that were passed down to us from our parents and other authority figures. It can be nurturing and caring, but it can also be critical and controlling.

Adult: This is where we take responsibility for our own actions. This ego state is rational and logical. It helps us to make objective decisions and solve problems.

Child: This is where we seek attention and care. This ego state is emotional and spontaneous. It's the part of us that feels emotion and experiences both joy and sadness.

Now, we all know someone who never seems to grow out of their Child role. They throw tantrums, demand attention and can't seem to take care of themselves. And let's not forget those whom we can always rely on to play the Parent role, controlling and micromanaging others - just think about what plays out around the dinner table on Christmas Day; it's always telling!

The aim, of course, is to be the Adult in our relationships. This means taking responsibility for our emotions and actions, communicating effectively and being respectful of others. When both people in a relationship, at home or at work, communicate from their Adult ego state, they are able to deal with complex issues objectively, without blame and with greater ease.

It's important to recognise that each person's ego state will change depending on the situation. For example, if a person feels threatened or vulnerable, they may shift into their Child ego state and become emotional. Alternatively, if someone is feeling particularly authoritative, they may shift into their Parent ego state and become controlling. We are all human and this isn't about right or wrong.

However, as divas and therefore role models, we need to own our shit. This means:

- Striving to recognise and minimise the negative impact of our Parent and Child ego states (not forgetting that they have many positives too).
- Recognising that behind every frustrating behaviour is a positive intent, e.g. to protect ourselves from getting hurt.
- Recognising that people have the capacity to change their ways.
- Communicating with others, ideally, Adult > Adult.
- Approaching conversations with an open mind, listening carefully to the other person's perspective and responding in a calm and rational manner.

Think about the role you play in your relationships:

- Are you the Parent, Adult or Child?
- How does the role you play differ depending on who you are with?
- What differences do you notice? For example between home or work.

WHAT ARE YOUR STRENGTHS?

My own process of getting to know myself began with this very question. I'd just been promoted and my new Line Manager sat me down, looked at me and said, 'So what are your strengths?' I paused, then paused some more. Eventually, he put me out of my misery and said something like, 'You've no idea what I'm talking about, do you?' And I didn't. It's hard to believe now. Helping people to uncover their strengths and discover the things that give them energy has become a big part of my work. I've worked with school-age kids, parents, teachers, people returning to work after parental leave, people going for promotions, newly promoted people, people retiring and people who are searching for a bit more fulfilment and joy in their lives. Knowing what I bring to the table has become part of my 'brand', I suppose. It's also a big part of what I believe powers a diva. That feeling of self-worth and self-assurance that comes from knowing what I have to offer others. Not in a hedonistic or egotistical way, but a way in which I'm focused on how I can *do* good rather than how I can *be* good.

Here's what you need to know about strengths:

Strengths are underlying qualities that energise you and that you are great at or have the potential to become great at - Dr Paul Brewerton, Founder of Strengthscope

Wow. This was a big eye-opener for me. You mean my strengths aren't the things I'm good at? Well, they are things that you are good at, but here is the important distinction; they are also the things that give you energy. They are the things that leave you feeling amazing, energised and ready to go back for more. And because you enjoy them, you probably spend more time using them and therefore naturally become good at them.

Of course, it's possible to be good at something that doesn't give you energy. Here's a story that's a bit dull but makes my point. I use the example of someone who is skilled at creating spreadsheets. I couldn't think of anything worse, but stick with me. Let's call them Deborah. Deborah can do all the fancy formulas and can whip up a spreadsheet faster than you can say, *You're 30! Why did your parents name you Deborah?* Whereas it might take the person next to them hours, Debs can do it in minutes. So, what happens typically in a work setting when somebody shows a talent for something? Well, they tend to get more of it, *Oh, could you just do this for me? You're so much better at it than I am.* The trouble is, as good as Deborah is at making spreadsheets, she goes home every evening and wants to poke her eyes out. She's miserable. In fact, she would love nothing more than to move to a place where spreadsheets don't exist and live an off-grid life herding goats (you live your best life, Debs). But word of Deborah's talent has spread around the office and before she knows it, she's being offered a new job, 'Head of Spreadsheets'. Without knowing any better, Debs takes the job. What happens? She's never heard of again and the goats go un-herded. I mean, she was heard from again; it's just that people referred to her as the crazy lady hiding by the photocopier.

What's this all about? DON'T BE LIKE DEBORAH.

Instead, arm yourself with the knowledge and insight that helps you to make better choices about how you spend your precious time. If you spend more of your time operating in your areas of strength, then trust me, you will be all the happier and more fulfilled for it. Don't be a Debby Downer.

IDENTIFYING YOUR STRENGTHS

So, if you don't want to end up like Debs, how do you begin to find out what your strengths are? It couldn't be simpler. Here are some strategies you could use:

- Think about the tasks that leave you feeling good afterwards - what are they?
- Think about a time when you were so immersed in what you were doing that you completely lost track of time, when you were so in the flow of things that you could've been on another planet - what were you doing?
- Ask the people closest to you what they think your greatest strengths are. There's an activity

in the chapter titled 'Confidence' called 'Read Your Fan Mail'. This can help here.

· Keep a diary. Make a note of what you are doing each time you are left feeling super energised and enthused. At the end of each week, look back over it and see if you can spot any themes emerging.

· Or look at this list of words I'm about to show you and see which you are drawn to.

Before we start, remember that this isn't about skill or competency; this is about what you enjoy doing. Don't be tempted to select some words because you feel you should - divas don't deal with 'should'. Nobody is going to check your work, so you can choose what you like, but try and go with your heart and gut on this one - keep your head out of it for now.

Understanding our strengths provides a foundation and a rock for our decision making, often closely aligned to our values. They can help us get clarity on the work we want to do (and not do), and they can change the nature of the conversations we have for the better! - Maria Salkeld, Quirky Bird Strengths

KNOWING YOURSELF

Creativity	Forgiveness
Curiosity	Empathy
Self-Development	Negotiation
Open-Mindedness	Modesty
Perspective	Self-Control
Courage	Gratitude
Authenticity	Hope
Bravery	Spirituality
Persistence	Decision Making
Kindness	Adaptability
Love	Getting Results
Social Intelligence	Logic
Fairness	Detail Focus
Leadership	Strategy
Teamwork	Optimism
Collaboration	Tenacity
Relationship Building	Self-Confidence

Got your list? Great. Now see if you can get it down to somewhere between 5 and 10, any more and it's hard to remember them. The idea is, should you be asked, you will be able to reel them off; that's more difficult if you've got 20. To help get them down, you might want to think about which strengths are particularly helpful to you in your life or work right now. Applying context is often a helpful way of bringing them to life. For example, right now I'm writing this book - so out of all of my strengths, Creativity, Action Focus and Detail are going to be particularly helpful for me.

What did you do as a child that made the hours pass like minutes? Herein lies the key to your earthly pursuit - Carl Jung

WATCH YOUR STEP

It is possible to have too much of a good thing. If you don't keep your strengths in check, then they can trip you up. Take one of your strengths and imagine that you set it to the max. You're living your best life, doing your thing and paying little attention to what's going on around you. What might the unintended negative consequences of your actions be on the people around you?

Here's one of my examples. 'Decision Making' is one of my top strengths. It gives me tonnes of energy and

I love it. So there I am, dialling it up to 100%, making decisions left and right centre. *Right, we just need to do X. OK, do X and then do X. I know what to do, we'll do X.* If I'm carrying on like this, how might the people around me be feeling at that moment? I'd hope inspired, but in truth, probably a bit shit. I'm not listening to them; they might as well not be there for all I care. I'm not doing it on purpose, I know what needs to be done and I just want it done. Now if I'm working for myself, that's probably not a problem. But if I'm relying on the support of others, I'm in trouble. Not only am I going to annoy people, but when people feel that they aren't heard or valued, they'll leave. So, I have to keep it in check. I do this by not letting myself get too overexcited and by making a point of asking at least two other people what they think we should do before I go in with my view. Most of the time the results have been all the better for it. Another example is a friend of mine who is the kindest, most compassionate and most caring person I've ever met. She would do anything for anybody, and she does. The unintended negative consequence in her case is that she puts everybody else's needs above her own and fails to take time for herself to rest and recover.

- In what ways could/do your strengths trip you up?
- What can you do to minimise the negative impact on yourself or others?

YOU CAN BE MORE THAN ONE THING

Breaking news. You can be more than one thing. Nobody pigeon-holes a diva. You can be a good, kind person *and* be a bit of a bitch sometimes. You can be self-assured and self-confident *and* be humble and non-assuming. You can be caring and compassionate and still want to tell others to shut the f*ck up. This big old world would have us believe that things need to be either one thing or another. Good or bad, black or white, right or wrong, male or female, gay or straight. This binary way of thinking makes it easier for us to process what we are experiencing. Humans like certainty; there is safety in certainty. You see it, you label it, there's little to no ambiguity, you feel safer about that thing you are experiencing and so you move on to the next. But it doesn't work like that. As soon as you realise that you don't need to fit a mould, hell, you are the mould - you are free, dear Diva, to live your life and do your thing. Relish in every bit of what makes you, you. Don't feel bad or ashamed if from time to time, your thoughts and actions don't line up with your view, or anybody else's for that matter, of what or how you 'should' be. It's pre-historic programming that doesn't serve us as we are today. It's the Windows 95 of the brain - and that shit ran on dial-up.

- In what ways does 'one thing thinking' hold you back?
- What would be possible if you chose to think about things a bit differently?

WHAT'S LED YOU TO BECOME THE PERSON YOU ARE TODAY?

You will never meet an interesting person who hasn't suffered. Suffering, like joy, is part of the human experience. And within it can be found valuable wisdom and insight.

Chances are you've had your fair share of shit. Maybe you've had more than your fair share. Perhaps you're still going through it. When you go through tough times, you learn things. You learn about yourself, you learn about what's important, you learn not to make the same mistake again, you learn not to take people or things for granted and you learn to make the most of what and who you have around you. The bad stuff you've experienced in your life has shaped you and made you who you are today, just as much as the good stuff has. The important distinction here is that whilst those 'not so good' experiences will have shaped you, they don't define you. They are, however, an important part of your story that can't and shouldn't be untold.

- What's the toughest thing you've come through?
- How has that shaped who you are today?
- What lessons did it teach you?
- In what way are those lessons benefiting you and those around you today?

You grow through the things you go through.

FINDING YOUR 'WHY' - STRIVING AND NEVER ARRIVING

You know, people can become obsessed with searching for meaning in their life. Why am I here? What's my life's purpose? I'll say the same thing to you as I've said to countless people over the years. To set out to find your purpose is to miss the point. Your purpose isn't something you find; it's something that finds you. When you understand yourself, you know what drives you, what makes you tick, you understand your triggers and your switches and you begin to spend more of your time doing the things that give you energy, something happens. You begin to work in alignment with yourself, rather than in opposition. More so, you begin to work in alignment with the universe and your higher self. This is the place to be. Only when you are out there, playing the field, being unapologetically you and not being a dick to people, will things start to make sense. Like the show Catchphrase, the tiles begin to disappear revealing the hidden picture underneath. Sitting and waiting for it to reveal itself to you won't do shit. Get out there, be you and try some stuff. Some things will work for you and some won't. With each 'won't', you're being directed closer and closer to something that will. In those moments, trust that when things don't work out, it's because the universe has something else planned for you - something better, but you've got to be in it to win it.

It took me almost 40 years to discover my purpose. I now understand it to be about sharing my knowledge, my skills and my story to empower others. I think I've always known it; it's always been a part of my work. But recently, the balance has shifted away from some of the other stuff to being much more focused on this specifically. Do I regret not finding it sooner? Yes. Would I have found it had I gone looking for it? No. I wasn't ready. I had to do the work to get ready.

So, get out there, dear Diva. Do your thing. Use your strengths; they are indications of your calling. Strut your stuff. And in time, all will be revealed.

So many people wish they knew why they were here, but don't make the effort to understand their strengths and to go with their intuition. Instead, the purpose-less person looks to others for instructions on how to live their life – It's important to not become obsessed with identifying purpose; let it be what it is. It already exists inside you – Tyler Henry

KNOW WHAT YOU STAND FOR

Knowing what you stand for is important when it comes to understanding yourself. These are the values that you live your life by. They determine how you think, the decisions you make and therefore the results that you get. They help you choose your battles, not just with others but with yourself too, and they play a big part in your relationships. On the flip side, they define the things that you won't tolerate, the behaviours and actions which to you, aren't acceptable.

Take a look at the chapter titled 'Standing Up For Yourself' to discover what it is you stand for.

ALL IS NOT AS IT SEEMS

The thing about being unique is that we each process, and therefore experience, the world differently. A hundred people could experience the exact same thing and every person's account of it will be different. Isn't that fabulous? This is why I bang on about there being no such thing as right or wrong, it's all about the P's: Perspective, Processing and Perception. Do you remember the photo of Prince William supposedly giving the paparazzi the middle finger? If you haven't seen it, then Google it. From the angle at which the photograph was taken, that's exactly what it appeared to be. Until a photograph was released which was taken at the exact same time, only this time front on. He wasn't just holding one finger up; he was holding up three. There was outrage; people were saying all sorts of things about him.

The thing is, our brains can't take in everything that's around us. There's just too much to notice. Sights, smells, textures, touch, taste, and that's just the external stuff. You then layer on thoughts, feelings, emotions, memories, and self-talk and I need to lay down just thinking about it. Have you ever arrived at work and had zero recollection of how you got there? Have you ever chatted about a TV programme with someone and thought, *Hmm, I interpreted that totally differently?* To deal with the constant barrage of stuff coming at us, our brains have developed a filtering system. Think of it as your inbuilt personal assistant, sorting around two million bits of information every second - damn, they're good. This PA is a godsend because without them, you wouldn't be able to keep up; you'd have a meltdown. But if the PA isn't set up right, if they haven't been given the proper training, if they don't know which messages you want passed on and which need to go straight into the trash, then you can easily start to find that the stuff that's being presented to you isn't the stuff that you want and the stuff you want has been tossed in the trash. Your PA, let's call them Todd, organises your sensory data in three ways:

Delete: That's not important - trash. *Mum, Mum, did you see? We just drove past a horse. Did we? That's nice.* Eyes on the road.

Distort: We misrepresent reality. *Oh my god, spider, get it out, get it out!* The spider isn't going to harm you; look at it, it's tiny.

Generalise: We draw conclusions based on our prior experiences and the beliefs that we hold about ourselves and others. *No, I can't do that. I tried before and it didn't work.* Come on now.

The longer the PA is in the job, the quicker they get to know what goes where and they become complacent. *I've always put that there, so that's where it goes.* They question less, they spend less time consciously analysing and more time just filing stuff away where they think it should go.

My point here is merely to say don't trust everything you think you know about yourself and the world. Be curious, seek out different points of view and be open to the idea that things might not be as they seem. Also, keep your PA in check. Even Todd should have a bi-annual review. Sit them down, check they are doing things the way you'd like them to be done, give them some more training if you need to and if required, give them a sharp talking to.

Being a diva means:

- Taking responsibility for how you view the world around you.
- Knowing how your filters, your beliefs and your

habits influence your behaviour.
- Being open to the idea that multiple 'truths' exist and that your reality is different to mine, and that's OK.
- Knowing that your way of thinking, being and doing is different to everybody else's, not right or wrong - just different.

Psychologically speaking, we see the world not as it is, but rather as we are - through our filters and biases. Do yourself a favour and clean your glasses once in a while (metaphorically speaking).

JUST BECAUSE YOU THINK IT DOESN'T MEAN IT'S TRUE

I've shared that one of the ways that we filter information is through our beliefs - the things that we perceive to be true about ourselves, others and the world in general. What's good or bad, what's right or wrong, what we can and can't achieve, how we 'should' be. Beliefs are nothing more than thoughts repeated. You tell yourself something often enough, you start to believe it. Our beliefs have the power to either propel us to success or to keep us small, to limit us. Identifying and then calling 'Billy Bullshit' on those beliefs that are keeping you small is a big part of what gives a diva their confidence and self-assurance. It's also important when it comes to achieving the stuff that you want, that you deserve and that you are worthy of.

What we don't transform, we transmit. Do the work needed to work through it, or it'll show - often at the most inconvenient of times.

Check out the chapter titled 'Self-Sabotage' to learn more about the beliefs you hold about yourself and the world.

CREATIVITY

One such belief that far too many people hold about themselves is that they aren't creative. Being a creative kinda bitch, I have to say something about this; I'll keep this short and sweet. Whether you believe it or not, you are creative. We all hold creative power. Every single one of us. You don't have to be some great artist to be creative; you can be creative in all sorts of ways. You might like to solve problems or fix things - that's being creative. You might like to read or write - that's being creative. You might like to daydream - that's being creative. You might like to dress in a certain way or think about how you match certain items and colours - that's being creative. Look around you. Everything you see has creativity running through it, including you.

It makes me cross when I meet people who say they aren't creative. I look at them and say, 'That necklace you're wearing, those earrings, that choice of lippy, that bag you've chosen to carry today, is that not expressing yourself creatively?' A belief is nothing more than a thought repeated (I will have this written on my gravestone, I'm sure). The more you tell yourself that you aren't creative, the more you start to believe it. Accept that you are - and you will be.

If you believed that you were creative, what would you attempt that you haven't so far?

CELEBRATE WHO YOU ARE

There's only one of you, dear Diva. They broke the mould when you were made. You're one of a kind. You're amazing. I want you to feel good about everything that you are, everything you have been and everything that you are becoming. You deserve all that this world has to offer you. But to get the most out of your precious time here, you need to start celebrating everything that makes you who you are.

The thing that people don't realise is that by trying to stand out, they become just the same as everybody else. Just do you.

Be you. Speak your mind. Do what makes you happy. Play, have fun, make mistakes and fail forward. Don't you dare rob the world of the light that you have to offer. If you won't do it for yourself, do it for the fans. Otherwise, know that I will find you.

YOUR BAD BITCH BOARD

Don't forget to write down everything that you are learning, unlearning and remembering about yourself on your Bad Bitch Board. You will find it in the chapter titled 'Confidence', and it acts as a reminder of who you are and what makes you unique.

Knowing yourself is the beginning of all wisdom - Aristotle

CHAPTER THREE

BUILD YOUR ENTOURAGE

A diva knows that it's not what you know, but who you know - and who knows you.

BUILD YOUR ENTOURAGE

Yes, you heard me, your entourage. They aren't just for Hollywood's rich and famous, you know. You can, and I would argue should, have an entourage of your very own. No diva is complete without a team of people behind them cheering them on, pushing them forward and willing them to do well.

Your entourage is made up of people who have valuable traits, knowledge, advice, skills and connections that can benefit you, either in your career or in helping you achieve your goals. It should also include people with characteristics and behaviours that you admire. Having positive, high-vibe, can-do people around you is just as important as having people with valuable knowledge and connections. But this isn't all about taking. True divas give as much as they receive and so in exchange, you return the favour. They help you achieve your goals and you help them achieve theirs. It's important to recognise early on, therefore, that it's not all about you. The more you go out of your way to help somebody else, the more likely it will be that they will do the same for you, perhaps when you need it the most. It can be helpful then to think about these relationships as if each were a bank account (this is true for any of your relationships). For a healthy and productive relationship to exist, you have to deposit into each account as much as you withdraw. People aren't stupid; think about your own experiences of being used or taken advantage of. You will have picked up early on that something didn't feel right. And once that damage is done, it's pretty hard to repair. Relationship-wise, consistently taking out more than you put in, is likely to cost you that relationship. This cost might affect you in all sorts of ways, least of all in the pursuit of your goals. If this sounds like it requires some work, then you'd be right. The rewards, however, far outweigh the effort - if you get it right.

Tips for building your entourage:

- Look for positive people with good energy. Negative energy will only lower your vibe.
- Don't be a dick. Be nice to everyone you meet; you never know when or how their 'entourage potential' might reveal itself.
- Don't make it all about you. When you meet somebody, take an interest, be curious and ask them about themselves. That way you are far more likely to uncover common ground and mutual interests.
- Start by asking yourself, How could I be of help to this person? You could share information, offer to connect them with somebody you know who could help them or offer your own services to them. It's amazing what a random act of kindness can achieve in the long run. I stand by this quote by the incredible poet Maya Angelou, *'People will forget what you said, people will forget what you did, but people will*

never forget how you made them feel.'

- We're all dealing with a lot. So, when somebody goes out of their way to help you, even in a small way, thank them. Show them that you are grateful and even better still, share the impact of their generosity by telling them about the difference it made to you.
- Check in with people. If you haven't spoken to somebody for a while, call them. Ask how they are doing. It's nice to know that you are on somebody's mind and that someone cares enough about you to pick up the phone and see how you are doing, without any agenda.
- Karma's a bitch. Watch what you say about people, especially those who have helped you get where you are. Nothing travels faster than a disloyal tongue - that shit's light-speed.
- If you say you're going to do something, then do it. If someone has to chase you, you've already lost. In my own experience, nothing signals a doomed relationship more so than unreliability. As the absolutely fabulous Dame Judi Dench once said, *'If you said yes, then you bloody well do the job.'* This is particularly true when it comes to accepting people's event invitations. If you are in two minds, then it's always better to politely decline and then find that you are able to attend after all, than to accept, only to pull out later.

- Never forget who has helped you along the way. If you haven't made your gratitude clear to them, then write them some fan mail and let them know.
- When you mess up, own it. I don't think there's anything more to be said here, really.
- When it comes to your entourage, account regularly. Do your checks and balances, making sure that your accounts are healthy and that you've all your bases covered.

Examples of Deposits:

- Offering your help and support.
- Keeping your promises.
- Showing loyalty.
- Following through with your commitments.
- Saying hi once in a while - without an agenda.
- Owning up and saying sorry when required.

Examples of Withdrawals:

- Breaking promises.
- Placing blame.
- Being unkind/discourteous.
- Being critical.
- Blanking.
- Being defensive.

WHO'S ON YOUR TEAM?

Think about the following types of people in your life and consider these questions:

- Who do you turn to?
- How do they help you? What do you offer them in return?
- Where do you have gaps? Where could you begin to fill them?
- Are you depositing at least as much as you are taking out?

WING / HYPE PEOPLE

These are the people who have got your back no matter what. When you need a boost, they are right there beside you. They're your biggest fans. They build you up, know just the right words to say to get you hyped and speak your name positively even when you aren't in the room. They're high-vibe people whose positive energy is good to be around. It tops you up - ready to go out there and do your thing. This group of people is so important. They don't come around all that often; these relationships are forged over time and through shared experiences. Don't take their kindness and support for granted and most definitely don't underestimate their value on the basis that they might not have some of the skills or connections that other members of your entourage do. If you do, then there will come a time when you trip, you will look around, and there will be nobody there to pick you up.

ROLE MODELS

These are people whom you look up to and aspire to be like. They might have done the things that you want to do, or it might be that they have mastered certain behaviours and mindsets that you wish to develop yourself. They can offer advice, wisdom, learning and tips that will prove invaluable. These people have walked the very path that you are setting out on. They know every bump in the road, every twist and turn. They know what's lurking under the bridge or around the blind bend. Their advice is invaluable, so take note.

KNOWLEDGEABLE / SKILLED PEOPLE

You can't do it all alone and you certainly can't master all the skills, tools and techniques needed to support you in every area of your life and career. These people hold the knowledge or skills which you may need to call on from time to time. It might be practical stuff like somebody that is good with technology and can build you a website or, whatever it is you need in that department. Or it might be professional support like a coach or a therapist. Whomever they are and whatever you call on them for, know that they are important assets.

CONNECTED PEOPLE

There's a saying that it's not what you know; it's who you know. Relationships are the foundation on which we get things done. Think about the last time somebody senior joined your company. How long was it before old contacts of theirs showed up? It makes sense then that to make things happen, you need to surround yourself with people who know people. People who can set up an introduction, put in a good word, give you a name to go off or who will speak your name in the right circles.

NO BULLSHIT PEOPLE

When you start getting too big for your boots, these people will bring you back don't to Earth with a thud. Whilst you might not like it, these people are really important. Ego is the enemy of the diva and these folks are your first line of defence. When your diva strengths go into overdrive, your 'No Bullshit People' will be the first to put you back in your place. Whilst it might at times feel easier not to have these people around, don't underestimate their value. When your head is in the clouds, or you start going into a tailspin, these people will be there to gently but firmly course-correct you. They do so not because they like getting one over on you, but because they care for you and they want you to do well. Can you really call a friend a friend if they only ever agree with you? I think not.

It's very rarely what you know that propels you forward and almost always who you know - and who knows you.

A LESS SERIOUS TAKE ON YOUR ENTOURAGE

Adopting the 'A-Lister' definition of an entourage for just a moment...

A diva simply cannot be expected to navigate life alone. You need a trusty entourage behind you to handle all of life's pesky little details. Details that might otherwise distract you from being utterly fabulous. From carrying your bags to fixing your hair, your entourage is your life support system. So, if you want to keep up with the other divas in town, you'd better get building your squad, pronto.

OK, so getting a bit closer to reality for a moment, you probably already have an entourage and just don't realise it...

The friend who is always bumping into someone they know - **Agent**

The friend who is always on social media and whose phone is constantly pinging - **Publicist**

The friend who is super organised and has a spreadsheet for everything - **Manager**

The friend who always has something to say about your outfit - **Stylist**

The friend whose hair looks amazing, even though she only washes it once a month - **Hairdresser**

The friend who knows every line from Legally Blonde - **Lawyer**

The friend that's a good listener - **Coach / Therapist**

The friend that knows your coffee shop order - **Personal Assistant**

The friend with the Davina McCall dumbbells - **Personal Trainer**

That friend who drives her mini like it's a getaway car - **Driver**

Who will make your entourage?

Allowing others to take care of you is, in itself, an act of service.

OUTGROWING PEOPLE

I came to a realisation sometime in my early thirties that not everybody we care about is meant to stay in our lives forever. There's a practical element to this in that there comes a point where it becomes simply impossible to give attention to everybody we'd like to; there just aren't enough hours in the day or days in the year. Therefore decisions, conscious or unconscious, are made which results in some people fading out into the background, whilst others fade in. This, I can accept.

But there is another force at play here, one that sits less comfortably with me, and this is that as we grow into ourselves, as we settle into our being and begin to fill out our bodies (metaphorically), we can find ourselves outgrowing relationships and people whom for years before we would never have entertained not having in our lives. The foundation on which the relationship was forged was so solid, that to consider life without them felt akin to blasphemy.

The truth is people change. They grow. They evolve. They move on. We start off on the same path. We may go to school together; we may continue to be close as we begin to find our way in the world and then something happens. The space between us expands and the distance becomes more and more apparent.

Sometimes you don't get closure.
You just move on.

There can come a point wherein the only thing we have in common with a person is the past. A life that was but is no longer. Our priorities change, our interests change, what we want from life changes and so the conversation changes with it. Before we know it, we are left wondering what this is all about. Things don't feel the same. This isn't like it was. Can't we go back to how it was? The answer, of course, is no. We are only ever moving in one direction, dear Diva, forwards. Onward to the next thing and to the next. What we needed in the past may not be what we need for our journey into the future.

Baggage is heavy. To avoid breaking our backs, we must learn to let some things go.

I've found it helpful to think about this as though it were a theatrical production...

Some people are meant to stay in our lives from the very first scene until the last. From curtain up to curtain down. From opening night until the final performance.

Others take to the stage, say their piece, play their part and promptly exit stage left. A part never to be reprised.

Others who we expect to be around until the end, depart far sooner than expected. Their performance, although brief, is still revered as one of the greats.

Some appear just as we think we've got a firm grasp of the plot - only to surprise us with an unexpected twist.

There are those who we thought had long left the run, only to take up their role again, as if no time had passed at all.

And then we have ourselves. The lead. The headliner. The name above the title. With each performance, with each standing ovation, the good, the bad and the ugly reviews - we hone our craft. Every night, every line reveals something new. Each show is a rehearsal for the next. An opportunity to try something different. To take the part in a new direction, into uncharted territory. To make it our own.

As your life changes, so will your inner circle.

CHAPTER FOUR

STANDING UP FOR YOURSELF

A diva knows that asking for what they need is not 'being demanding'. It's sending a message that they matter too.

STANDING UP FOR YOURSELF

Here's the thing. Being a diva is about knowing what you will and will not tolerate. It's about knowing what is and isn't acceptable in terms of how we treat ourselves, how we treat others and how we allow others to treat us. Nobody has the right to mistreat, use and abuse you, dear Diva - not even you.

So, why is it that some people seem to have no problem at all standing up for themselves? How come some people can just say no, whilst others are exhausting themselves marching to the beat of somebody else's drum? How do some people manage to make time for the things they love and want, whilst others are working through endless lists of musts and shoulds? It's easy to tell somebody that they need to stand up for themselves, to say no more often, to place their needs above those of others just once in a while, to stop allowing themselves to be trampled over or to give themselves permission to put their oxygen mask on first before reaching to help others. But experience has taught me that this is much easier said than done. What's that all about? I have a few ideas...

PEOPLE PLEASING

If you've spent your whole life bending to the will of others, then of course change won't come easy. If we do something enough then it becomes a habit, if we tell ourselves something enough, it becomes a belief. If unchallenged, these habits and beliefs are then reinforced again and again over the years. Beliefs like, *If I say no, then people will think I'm not a nice person.* When these beliefs are perpetuated over time, they become like concrete roadblocks setting hard in the neural pathways of your brain, forcing you down unwanted paths and making alternative routes inaccessible. This makes different, more positive beliefs, hard to adopt. Imagine then that somebody comes along and says, *Well just say, no - it's that easy.* Well of course it's never 'that' easy. There's no quick fix, you can't go round, over or under. It starts with taking a chisel to those roadblocks, chipping away a bit at a time until new routes become accessible.

If any of this resonates with you, then know that taking a closer look at these beliefs can help. Name them, think about where they came from and then really challenge yourself as to whether they are true or indeed helpful. Ask yourself:

- What stories do I tell myself about my people-pleasing?
- What underlying beliefs about myself/the world do those stories reinforce?
- Where did they come from? A particular person? Relationship? Or period in my life?
- Are they true? What good do they do me?
- What would a more accurate and helpful version sound like?

Language is key. Notice the words you use - words power beliefs. Words like 'must', 'need' and 'should', if unchecked, have the power to perpetuate behaviours and beliefs without you even knowing, especially if you've been doing it for years, decades even, without clocking it. When you hear yourself say, *I need to...* STOP and ask yourself...Do I need to? Should I be doing...? Is that true? Is it helpful? What would happen if I didn't? What's the worst possible thing that could happen if I didn't? And how likely, really, is that to happen? Then spend that time and energy on yourself instead.

The other thing to bear in mind, and you might not want to hear this, is that with people pleasing, there is almost always a pay-off, meaning that there is something in it for you. You are getting something out of this exchange, which is one of the reasons why you will keep coming back for more. Even an innocent feeling of having done a good deed, of having helped somebody and feeling good about that, is enough to keep you coming back for more. It's perhaps an extreme comparison to make, but I liken it to the feeling that an addict might get from taking drugs or drinking alcohol. It's a dopamine high, and why would you stop if you are getting high off the back of this behaviour? The question I often ask people is, what is the cost to you if you don't stop? How about the other people in your life? What price will they pay?

It's important to remember that you are always at choice, meaning that you and you alone decide whether to be complicit in the story or whether you will choose a different one. A more helpful one. Choice is something that might not be familiar to you if you have consistently placed your needs below those of others and allowed yourself to be enslaved by the needs, musts and shoulds. Give it a go, it might be uncomfortable at first, but allow yourself to choose one thought over another, or one action over another. One small step forward is worth more than a thousand good intentions.

The problem with putting others first is that you teach them that you come second. Don't set yourself on fire to keep others warm.

SELF-WORTH

If you carry an underlying belief that you aren't worthy and that you don't have the right to be happy, to be taken care of and to place your needs above those of others - then of course you are going to find standing up for yourself tough.

Low self-worth should be a concern. Nobody should feel like they aren't worthy of all the glorious things this world has to offer and more. Of course, it's normal to have the odd wobble, to give yourself a talking to and get back on track, but if your lack of self-worth gets to the point where it is restricting how you live your life, then you need to check yourself before you wreck yourself. Get some advice from either your GP or a therapist. There is no shame in seeking support, after all, the most famous divas out there have their therapists on speed dial.

Respect yourself enough to say no often and f*ck off when required.

SIGNS OF LOW SELF-WORTH

- You are a habitual people-pleaser.
- You negate your own needs.
- You find accepting compliments excruciating.
- You frequently compare yourself to others and beat yourself up over inconsequential things.
- You speak about yourself unkindly, to yourself and to others.
- You frequently use self-deprecating humour. *Oh what am I like, I'm so stupid.*
- You have little faith in yourself and your abilities.
- You invest little to no time in learning about and developing yourself.
- You fail to set and maintain boundaries.
- You avoid the company of others on the grounds that you'll 'lower the vibe'.

If you sit in shit for too long, it stops smelling. So come the f*ck outta there – Jennifer Lewis

TIPS FOR BUILDING SELF-WORTH

- Notice your thoughts - how you think, feel and act, and intervene when this isn't aligned with how you want to be. See 'Knowing Yourself'.
- Practise positive self-talk. See 'Confidence'.
- Spend less time on social media. See 'Taking Care of Yourself'.
- Remind yourself that nobody is perfect. See 'Self-Sabotage'.
- Compliment yourself regularly. See 'Confidence'.
- Get to know yourself and find out what makes you tick. See 'Knowing Yourself'.
- Discover your strengths, the things that give you energy and leave you feeling good. See 'Knowing Yourself'.
- Build your Bad Bitch Board. See 'Confidence'.
- Set small and manageable goals and then celebrate your achievements, especially the small wins. See 'Goals'.
- Rely less on external validation and the nice things others have to say about you. Say nice things about yourself instead! See 'Confidence'.
- Make time for self-care. Eat, sleep and move well. See 'Taking Care of Yourself'.
- Connect with your higher self. See 'Spirituality'.

KNOWING WHAT YOU STAND FOR

If you already know what you stand for, great. If you are in any way unsure, then this next exercise is for you. Maybe it's never occurred to you to think about what it is you stand for, or perhaps it's been so long since you last stood up for yourself (or something/someone) that you've simply forgotten what's important to you. This is particularly true with people who have experienced prolonged abuse at the hands of another. Extended periods of wanting to please the perpetrator, attempting to keep them in a 'happy' state to avoid the consequences, to make sure their needs are met first and foremost, has meant that their own sense of self has been gradually eroded. It's also common among parents. So much focus has been placed on the needs of the child, to keep them alive and healthy, that the parent's needs become secondary.

Regardless of the cause, once you know what you stand for, you can set healthy boundaries for yourself that protect your own interests and that remind you that you are important and worthy too. You are so worthy, dear Diva - of it all.

If you don't stand for anything,
you'll fall for everything.

VALUES

The things that you stand for are called your values. Your values are the foundation on which you build and live your life. Yes, they really are that significant. They determine your sense of right and wrong, the decisions you make, your actions and therefore your results. When you live in alignment with your values, things feel 'right'. When you don't, you will know it. You will feel out of kilter, uneasy and dissatisfied.

You will have experienced times when a person, people or perhaps even a business has acted in a way that conflicts with your values. You might have thought, *I can't believe they've done that; I'd never act in that way.* Maybe you've found yourself in a position, perhaps at work, where you were asked to behave in a way that didn't align with your values. For example, being asked to send a strongly worded email when you value personal connection, harmony and kindness. You may have even found yourself unknowingly working for a company that was juxtaposed with your values. For example, working for a global, financially driven company when you value community, charity and freedom.

Your values steer your day-to-day life, most of the time unconsciously. They are the built-in sat-nav by which you navigate life - except that following this sat-nav will never lead you down the wrong road!

It's likely that you already have a sense of what your values might be. Labelling them is a powerful way of checking in with yourself when things don't quite feel right or when you need to make a decision - big or small. The activities that follow are helpful ways of gaining clarity on what your values are and the ways in which they both help you and, at times, get in your way.

The chances are, if I asked you to tell me what your values were, you'd stumble, or you'd at least need to give it some thought - that's only natural. It's typically only people who do this stuff for a living that can reel them off at the drop of a hat. That does have its benefits though. Being clear on your values can help you in many areas of your life, for example, choosing a life partner, making career choices, stating your point of view, picking your battles, working out why something or someone has annoyed you, etc.

Here are fifty examples of values. Some you might vibe with, others you won't; that's the whole point. This unique selection is partly what makes you who you are. How fabulous!

PART 1:

- Glance down the list on the next page and put a mark next to any values you feel are important to you.
- Once you've done a first pass, try to whittle them down to your top ten. Don't overthink it, trust your gut and avoid telling yourself unhelpful stories about what you do and don't choose. Stories like, if you don't choose kindness, that means that you aren't kind. It doesn't work like that; we are all more than one thing, dear Diva. Go to where you are drawn to most.
- Once you land on ten, whittle them down to your top five. This makes them easier to remember. But if you end up with more, that's fine too, especially if rule-breaking happens to be one of your values!
- If you don't vibe with some of the words, add your own! They need to feel as though they represent you through and through.

Acceptance	Honesty	Professionalism
Achievement	Humility	Punctuality
Ambition	Inclusion	Quality
Adventure	Innovation	Relationships
Bravery	Integrity	Reliability
Collaboration	Intuition	Respect
Creativity	Kindness	Responsibility
Curiosity	Knowledge	Safety
Empathy	Leadership	Security
Excellence	Loyalty	Spirituality
Fairness	Motivation	Stability
Family	Open Communication	Success
Friendship	Optimism	Tenacity
Flexibility	Passion	Time Management
Growth	Patience	Wealth
Happiness	Popularity	Wisdom
Hard Work	Power	Work-life Balance

Done? Great, so you now have a list of values - woohoo! The next part is figuring out what they mean to you and how they both help and, at times, get in your way.

Awareness = Choice. Once you know how your values impact your day-to-day life, you can make more informed choices about how you allow them to influence you and how you can use them to the max.

PART 2:

Here goes. For each of your values, ask yourself these questions:

- How does it feel when you are living in alignment with this value? Meaning that you are thinking and acting in a way that supports it.
- Where did it come from? Who in your past might have helped to shape it?
- Which behaviours of yours reinforce it?
- Which behaviours of yours conflict with it?
- How does this value help you day-to-day? What good does it do?
- How does this value hinder you/get in your way?
- How does this value inform how you behave around others?
- What are the warning signs that this value is being trampled on or that you are diverting from it?
- Who do you have around you who encourages or may share this same value?

- Who do you have around you who doesn't share this same value? It isn't a bad thing; we're all different. But knowing who they are might help you avoid unnecessary conflict.

KNOWING WHAT YOU WON'T STAND FOR

So, you know what you stand for, you know how your values help you day-to-day and you know how they can get in your way. You might even know a bit more about where your values came from and who, over time, has reinforced them. But being a diva means also knowing what you won't stand for and standing by that.

It's often much easier to figure out what we don't want or like:

- What can you absolutely not stand?
- Which behaviours in others really frustrate or annoy you?
- If you became Prime Minister tomorrow and had to ban five things to make the world a better place - what would they be?

If you don't take the reins, it's going to stay the same. Nothing's gonna change if you don't change it - Dolly Parton

YOUR DIVINE RIGHTS

If you're going to stand by the things that are important to you, then you have to believe that you have a divine right to do so and that others have that same right too. Even when those things differ from yours - and they will.

Remind yourself of your divine rights and if helpful, keep them to hand:

- I have the right to my own needs and feelings and to have them be as important as anyone else's.
- I have the right to experience my feelings and to express them if I want to.
- I have the right to not be held responsible for other people's feelings.
- I have the right to express my own opinions.
- I have the right to decide my own priorities.
- I have the right to be independent if I want to.
- I have the right to decide how I spend my time.
- I have the right to choose how I live my life.
- I have the right to change myself, my behaviours and my life.
- I have the right to change my mind.
- I have the right to make mistakes.
- I have the right to develop and express my talents and interests.
- I have the right to choose who I spend my time with.

- I have the right to choose who I share my body with.
- I have the right to be treated with dignity and respect by everyone I come into contact with.
- I have the right to be listened to respectfully.
- I have the right to ask for what I need.
- I have the right to say no.
- I have the right to set limits and boundaries.
- I have the right to walk away from relationships that I determine are not good for me.
- I have the right to have my boundaries respected.

Credit: Your Basic Human Rights, Barefoot Coaching

Asking for what you need, whether it's more money, time or space, isn't 'being assertive', it's exercising your divine right.

'NO.' IS A FULL SENTENCE

No = A small but mighty word which requires no further explanation or justification and should always be followed by a full stop. Other useful phrases include 'Not on your nelly' and 'Shove it up your arse'.

You have the right to say no and still be a good person. Did you hear that? A 'no' delivered gently but firmly and in your own interest is an act of kindness towards yourself. You also have the right to not have to explain or justify your 'no'. 'No' is a full sentence. I mean, you don't have to be rude. You could say, *No, that's not going to be possible, but I hope you find someone else. OK, see you, bye.* You also have the right not to feel guilty or worried about what happens next. You want to help people and you want to be kind; I get it. But you can't help everyone. Sometimes the line has to be drawn firmly, especially with those people who take advantage.

Let go, dear Diva – or be dragged.

Do you feel bad that some person wants to go on holiday and can't find anyone to take care of their dog? Do you know that you could do it, but it would mean cancelling your plans and priorities? Do you say no and then worry that they won't be able to find anyone? Tough tits. If you want to go abroad on holiday, don't have a dog. What's the worst that will happen? They have a staycation instead! Trust that people can and should take responsibility for their own shit. That's their business, not yours - stay out of it. If more people took responsibility for themselves and their actions, then the world would be a better place.

LOOK BACK TO MOVE FORWARD

Think about a time when you said *yes* too much:

- How did you end up feeling?
- What were the consequences for you and the people you love and care for?

The next time you are in an awkward position, ask yourself: If I say *yes* to this person, what will I be saying *no* to? Well, here are a few things:

- Your own needs, plans and priorities.
- Precious time with your partner, family and friends.
- Good times that you didn't even know you were going to have.
- Time to rest and recharge so that you can stay happy and healthy and be at your best for yourself and those you care about.
- Sleep.
- Your self-worth.

You know, humankind hasn't existed this long without learning to be canny, persuasive, to influence, negotiate and to get what we want. These skills can be used to do good or to serve our own selfish needs and desires. This means someone else gets to live their best life while you're left shovelling shit - their shit. Do yourself a favour and don't fall for that nonsense again.

BATTEN DOWN THE HATCHES, DAH-LING!

Imagine that you own the most beautiful, incredible mansion filled with priceless, one-of-a-kind artefacts - I'm talking about gilded stuff. What would happen if you left a window open one night? Perhaps not much; I mean you live in a nice area, there's a Waitrose. How about if you left a window and a door? What if you were to get complacent and before you know it all the doors and windows were left open? You can live in the nicest area with the most expensive council tax and you will still get your ass robbed. No question. The place is left wide open for people to waltz in like they own it, put their feet up on your sofa, eat your food, drink your wine and waltz right back out the door with a load of stuff that doesn't belong to them. And what makes it even more ridiculous is that you're standing there watching it happen. They are looking you in the eye and taking from you - and you are complicit. Do you think the insurance will pay out when you practically invited them in and fed and watered them? No.

YOU are the house, dear Diva. Those priceless objects are the things that you hold dear. They are your time, your energy, your values, everything that makes you who you are - one of a kind, priceless - gilded. The only way to stop people walking right in and taking from you under your nose is to batten down the hatches. Put locks on those doors, catches on those windows, set up CCTV monitoring and enable your early warning system.

The good news is that not everybody is out to take from you; most people aren't. But if your boundaries aren't set, then you'll find yourself one day needing them and they won't be there. Prevention is better than cure.

Complete these sentences:

- I will no longer allow...
- I choose not to spend time with people who...
- If my boundaries are violated, I will...
- If I'm asked to do something I don't want to, I will...
- Under no circumstances will I...

Anything you lose when you stand up for yourself isn't meant to stay.

FIVE THINGS TO KNOW ABOUT SETTING BOUNDARIES

1. To make people stand up and listen, you need to be clear and direct. Messages are easily lost or misinterpreted, so be specific about what you want to be different.

2. If people attempt to challenge the boundary you are putting in place, then just know how much it is needed in the first place.

3. Don't over explain or get into a debate about it. You don't owe anybody who is taking from you anything at all. It's not their business to ask why or seek information. It is what it is. Deal.

4. Stick to your guns. A boundary is only a boundary if it's reinforced. There's no point putting it in place if you aren't going to respect it.

5. When things feel tough and people are trying their best to take you for a fool, just remember why you needed this for yourself in the first place.

The only people who will complain about you setting boundaries are those who were benefiting when you had none.

ONE SIZE DOESN'T FIT ALL

Comparison is the thief of joy. We each have our own way of dealing with things. For some people, standing up for themselves will be loud, provocative and attention grabbing. But it doesn't have to be. Sometimes standing up for yourself means remaining silent. You don't need to explain or justify yourself, so why should you? You know yourself well enough to know that this situation doesn't require your precious attention or energy; it's better off spent elsewhere. You are confident and self-assured enough to just step away quietly and with grace.

How empowering it is to stay silent when they expect you to be enraged.

COURAGE

Courage is a funny old thing. For a long time, I believed that courage was something you either had or didn't have. I also thought it was big and brash, like a scene from Braveheart with the warriors putting on their armour and applying their slap. But my view on what it means to be courageous has totally changed as I've gotten older and hopefully wiser. Having courage doesn't mean being courageous all the time or that you have to behave or appear a certain way. Some of the most courageous people I know are the softest, kindest, good-hearted people - and at the same time they have gone through some of the most awful things a human being could experience. Things that you wouldn't wish on your worst enemy. And yet, they go on. They get up each morning, put on a smile and face the world. They carry on giving to others despite having what they deem most precious taken away from them. That is courage, dear Diva. It's not always about what's going on the outside. It's not always big and loud and obvious and gregarious. It's also soft, quiet, determined, gritty and resilient. True courage, real courage, comes from within. Often unheard and unseen. For this reason, if you and I were to sit down over coffee, our conversation about courage is likely to go something like this...

Me: Let's talk about courage. What do you think about it?

You: Well, I don't think I'm very courageous.

Me: Really? Why not?

You: Well, because of x, y, z.

Me: OK, tell me about some of the most difficult times in your life.

You: *Still talking 20 minutes later.*

Me: And you said you didn't think you were very courageous? What about all that?

You: ...Oh yeah.

Courage isn't having the strength to go on. It's going on when you don't have the strength.

135

YOU OK, BABE?

Ever wondered how you can spend time with some people and leave feeling good about yourself, whilst others leave you feeling a bit shit? Have you ever wondered why it is that some of your relationships at home or at work feel 50/50, whilst others feel more one-sided? How about when things don't go to plan? Who can you guarantee will play the blame game and who takes the, *It is what it is. Let's just find a way through it,* approach?

In his 1964 book 'Games People Play', Canadian Psychiatrist Eric Berne described four life positions that we may find ourselves in at any given time. These are:

- I'm OK - You're Not OK (It's your fault).
- I'm Not OK - You're OK (It's my fault).
- I'm Not OK - You're Not OK (We are both to blame).
- I'm OK - You're OK (It's nobody's fault. It simply is what it is).

Underpinning Berne's work was the concept that fundamentally, all human beings are 'OK'. Meaning that every life has value and is deserving, regardless of how that life is lived and the choices made. I extend this to include 'no life is more or less important than another'. This is possibly the most important differentiator between the divas of old and the new breed of diva - you and I. Old school divas believed they were above the average Joe - that they were better. The new breed of diva recognises that we are all created equal and that each of us is just doing our best to get by with what we have. As divas, we don't make it personal - ego has no place here. It's not all about me and it's not all about you. It simply 'is what it is' and we'll work it out together.

The only healthy life position, therefore is 'I'm OK and You're OK'. If we all felt like that a bit more often, then the world would be a brighter place. It's important to give some thought as to who leaves you feeling 'OK' and equally who leaves you feeling less than 'OK'. My instincts tell me that as you were reading this, some of those people came to mind. Trust your instincts here...I was going to write that nobody has the right to make you feel shit about yourself, like you're the one to blame - you're the problem. I stopped myself because it's important to know that nobody can 'make' you feel any sort of way. Emotions are merely suggestions as to how you might choose to feel. You don't have to go along with them. You are at choice. I suggest you use that choice to do a little spring cleaning, dear Diva. Whatever the season, it's out with the old and in with the new - *so long.*

When you blame and criticize others, you are avoiding some truth about yourself.
- Deepak Chopra

A BIT OF ROUGH AND TUMBLE

Now personally, I'm a fan of a bit of healthy conflict. This is something I've noticed about myself over the years. The word 'conflict' used to fill me with dread at the thought of raised voices and turn-taking slanging matches. What I've come to realise is that healthy conflict is an important part of relationships and that we can learn a lot about people by how they enter into conflict with us, the manner in which they treat us and how they conduct themselves during and afterwards. Whether this is healthy or not - you decide, I now don't fully enter into relationships with colleagues, ones in which I open myself up and share what I really think and feel, until we've had a bit of rough and tumble and we've come through it. Leadership experts would say that conflict is critical to creating high-performing teams. What good is a team who only ever agree with one another? Or worse, who disagree but don't say so. I think it's critical to any and all relationships. We can learn a lot about each other, for example:

- Will you always agree with me or are you willing to call out my poor behaviour for my own good?
- When you fundamentally disagree with me, will you share it openly, or will you talk behind my back?
- If you have something to say about me, will I hear it from you first or from others?
- Will you still treat me with respect even when we disagree?

- Can we keep the conversation adult > adult or will you turn it into a slanging match and resort to below-the-belt remarks?
- Can we say what needs to be said 'have it out' and then carry on as normal afterwards?
- Afterwards, will you go running and tell tales to the boss? Or does this stay between us?
- Does our disagreement bring us closer together or further apart?

Ask yourself:

- What is your relationship with conflict like?
- What negative experiences have you had that make you weary of entering into healthy conflict?
- What stories do you tell yourself about entering into conflict? E.g. *They will think I'm aggressive,* etc.
- What more affirming and positive stories could you tell yourself?

A life without conflict is a life lived in solitude.
– Victoria L Adenson

CALLING OUT POOR BEHAVIOUR

The reality is we can't conduct our diva business without standing up for ourselves and for others. That will, at times, require us to put our big person pants on and have conversations that we may not like having, but ultimately need to have. When somebody violates your boundaries or treats you unkindly, you have two options. You either speak to them about it or vow never to cross paths with them again. The latter isn't always possible and my preference has always been to talk it through. Not argue, point fingers or blame - but talk it through. Being a diva means assuming positive intent and then having people prove you right. There's a chance they didn't know what they were doing. They were clumsy; they didn't think before they opened their mouth. There could be any number of reasons and causes. You can either tell yourself all sorts of stories about what was or wasn't meant, or you can simply talk to them.

Just because you are being firm, doesn't mean you're being rude. Just because you are being direct, doesn't mean you are being aggressive. Standing up for yourself is not equal to doing harm - Psychology Peers

COURAGEOUS CONVERSATIONS

There is a really simple way of structuring a conversation with someone whose words, behaviours or actions have impacted negatively on you. You owe it to yourself to set and maintain boundaries around what you will and won't tolerate from others. Yes, if you aren't used to having this type of conversation, then it might feel scary. Just know that you are far more likely to regret not having a conversation than having it:

WHEN YOU: Describe the thing the person said or did. Focus only on observed behaviours or actions, not hearsay. Be specific - include when and where.

I FELT: Describe the feeling and reaction you had and own it. Don't say, *You made me feel...* because nobody can make you feel anything. You always have a choice. The power of this approach lies within personal ownership, which can't be disputed.

BECAUSE: This is where you share your feelings and the reason you reacted as you did. This bit is optional!

WHAT I'D LIKE IS: This is the point where you clearly tell the person the alternative behaviour or action that you'd like instead.

WHAT DO YOU THINK? This is where you check it out with them and mutually agree on the way forward.

Practise. Practise. Practise. Until it comes naturally.

—CHAPTER FIVE—

GOALS

*A diva knows that nothing is impossible,
because the word itself says, 'I'm possible'.*

GOALS

A diva knows that the world is their oyster. Whatever they put their mind to, they can achieve through hard work, grit and determination. If you've arrived here looking for a secret recipe to success, a side door to abundance, you won't find it - believe me, I've looked. What I've come to realise is that the one thing that differentiates those people who make their dreams come true from those that don't, is that those that do aren't put off by setbacks. They are clear about what it is they want; they know that there will be bumps along the way and so they expect and prepare for them. They understand that as frustrating as setbacks can be, they are an important and necessary part of the process. Setbacks teach us what we need to learn. They help to finesse the final product and make the taste of success all the sweeter.

When it comes to making your dreams come true, you have to start by knowing what you want. Create a clear goal in your mind, something to aim for and something to measure your progress against as you go out there and make it happen. Goals are as much about how you want to *be* as they are about what you want to *do*. The two are intrinsically linked. To achieve a different outcome, you have to do something different, which may require a new way of thinking, behaving and being.

If you want something you've never had, you
need to do something you've never done.
- Barbra Streisand

BELIEVE THAT YOU ARE WORTHY

Sometimes, doing the thing that you've never done before means believing that you are worthy of the things you desire, dear Diva. Believe me when I say that you are worthy beyond words. Worthy of everything that this life has to offer you and then some. You are the universe in human form, made of stardust that has existed in the galaxy for billions of years before it took form in who you are today. You are yourself, a manifestation of divine cosmic creation. The universe runs through you. You are everything that ever has and ever will exist. Now you are really going to turn around and tell me that you aren't worthy? Bitch, please!

FINDING YOUR WHY

Purpose breathes life into everything we do,
solidifying and manifesting that which all
starts on an internal level - Tyler Henry

Purpose is crucial. Purpose gives life to everything you do and brings into existence everything that you desire for yourself. Knowing why it is that you want to achieve this thing and then being clear about how it will benefit you, will not only keep you motivated on your journey to success, but will increase your chances of seeing it through. When you hit bumps in the road, you will be able to remind yourself of the higher purpose behind your actions, a sort of beacon or north star that will steady your ship and see you safely on your way again. Ask yourself:

- Why am I doing this?
- Who will I become after doing this?

The two most important days in your life are the day you were born and the day you find out why - Mark Twain

THE FIVE WHYS

Self-enquiry is a powerful thing, dear Diva. It's surprising what you can find out about yourself by taking the time to ask a simple question like, why? How often do you do that? Check in with yourself, I mean. You might ask yourself how you are feeling that day, what you are thinking, why something has annoyed you or even what's important to you at any given moment. If you do, then great. You're working in alignment with yourself; you are in tune with your thoughts, feelings and needs. If you don't so much, then give it a go - you'll be better off for it and what you learn might just surprise you.

GOALS

When it comes to why you want to achieve something, the 'why' takes on a whole new meaning. It allows you to delve deeper into that gorgeous and precious mind of yours, to tap into your subconscious and to get to the heart of what's going on. Getting to the nub of it allows you to elevate your goals to a whole new level. Suddenly, 'my goal is to save enough money to afford a deposit on a house' becomes 'my goal is to give my kids the safety and security that I didn't have growing up.' Notice the difference? If you were in their shoes, which would you be more determined to make happen?

When it comes to getting to the heart of the matter, it's said that the simple and unassuming question 'why' should be asked five times. Give it a go for yourself. You might like to speak it aloud or you might prefer to write your answers down. Either way, prepare to hear some stuff from yourself that you weren't expecting. Here's an example. Remember that the questions you ask yourself will be specific to your situation:

- Start with stating your goal. *I want to get a new job by the end of the year.*
- Why do I want to get a new job? *Because I'm unhappy in my current job.*
- Why am I unhappy in my current job? *Because I don't feel like I'm going anywhere.*
- Why is going somewhere important to me? *Because I feel like I have so much more to give*

     and my strengths and skills aren't being used where I am.

- Why is being able to use my strengths and skills important to me? *Because despite being really talented, my parents spent their whole life doing work that they hated because they didn't believe they could do any better, and I don't want to end up like them.*
- Why don't I want to be like my parents? *Because I don't want to work my whole life doing something I hate and then retire. I want to be able to do work that makes me happy and that brings me joy. I want to be able to do what they couldn't...I want to make music.*

Boom. See what happened there? In five simple whys, we went from wanting a new job because we were unhappy, to wanting to do work that makes use of our strengths and skills and brings us joy. In the end, we weren't really pursuing a new job at all. We were pursuing a dream, a dream to make music and to show our parents that it is possible to have a career doing what we love. Now, jacking it all in and starting a new career as a musician will take work and requires a lot of thought and planning - it won't happen overnight. But we've got to the nub of our unhappiness at work and we've unearthed the real aim and desire that was floating around in our unconscious, that we might have clocked before and thought, *It's just a silly dream; everyone has those,* but might not have realised how significantly that desire was playing out in our day-to-day lives. What would have happened if we'd stuck with the original goal and gotten ourselves a new job by the end of the year? We'd be in this same position, feeling dissatisfied with little idea of what was really behind that feeling. Try it. Imagine you're being interviewed by your favourite glossy magazine and have fun with it.

WHO AM I DOING IT FOR?

I got no man; I got no lady. I do it for myself.
- Celine Dion

This may sound like an obvious question, but for whom you want to achieve your goal is important. You have to really want it and you have to want it for the right reasons.

There are two types of motivation:

INTRINSIC: This is about doing something because you want to do it. For example, it will bring you joy, or it will be personally rewarding for you in some way. Like Celine, you're doing it for yourself.

EXTRINSIC: This is about doing something because you feel like you 'should'. For example, in order to please someone or support somebody else's agenda. Essentially, you're doing it for somebody else.

Now, don't get me wrong. Extrinsic motivation isn't all bad. External rewards can be useful in making stuff happen and getting shit done. I often advise people to share their goals with others as a way of helping them to be held accountable for doing what they said they would do. The problem comes if your core reason for taking action to bring about change is being driven by something or someone other than yourself. How likely will you be to see it through?

As a diva, you work for one person and one person only - yourself.

TOWARDS OR AWAY FROM?

One of the things that makes humankind so bloomin' amazing, I think anyway, is how despite being so alike and sharing 99.9% of our DNA, in fact - we are all so uniquely different. All 8 billion of us are driven by different things: love, money, peace, family, fame, etc. We each have a different set of values. We have differing interests, styles, hobbies, passions, loves and goals, and so it stands that we are each motivated differently. Depending on the goal, you might either be motivated towards something, for example, being motivated towards making music and having a job that really allows you to use your strengths or skills. Or you might be motivated away from something, for example, not ending up like your parents. Depending on your own circumstances, you may be drawn to one, more so than the other - or being motivated by both is fine too!

Ask yourself, what's really motivating me here - towards pleasure? Or away from pain?

TWO FUTURES

There's an exercise that I love that allows you to experience and really feel what your life would be like in two different futures. On the one hand, you keep on doing what you've always done, and you get what you've always got. What would that be like? What price do you pay for taking no action? On the other hand, you do something different, you bring about the change that you want, and you get something new. Now how would that feel? What are you doing now that you couldn't before? Here's how it works:

You choose the time frame. It could be six months' time, a year, five, ten - whatever works for you.

STEP 1: Imagine two versions of yourself sitting in front of you. The version of you on your left has taken no action towards achieving your goal. The version to your right has not only taken action, but they've smashed it and have achieved everything you wanted.

STEP 2: Focussing on the person to your left (no action):

- What do you notice about them?
- How do they appear?
- What is life like for them?
- What have been the costs to them and those around them of having taken no action towards their goals?

As uncomfortable as it may be, try and spend some time here. You might even like to step into their shoes and really feel what they are feeling - perhaps disappointment, sadness, or regret. Don't move on until you've really explored what this potential future would be like for you.

STEP 3: Now turn your focus to the person on your right (smashed it). Ask yourself the same questions:

- What do you notice about them?
- How do they appear?
- What is life like for them?
- This time, what have been the benefits to them and those around them of having achieved what you wanted to achieve?
- What are they doing now that wasn't possible before?

Once you've lapped up the joy and positivity, step into

their shoes and ask yourself:

- How does it feel to be 'future me'? Really spend some time here, revel in your success and feel that sense of pride and achievement.
- How did I do it? How did I make it happen?
- What steps did I take?
- When things got tough, how did I stay motivated?
- Who helped me?

STEP 4: When you've had enough, step back into your 'today' shoes:

- What's the first thing you are going to do to move closer towards your goal?

Done. See? It's gorgeous. So much insight and valuable motivation can be derived by exploring these two parallel futures. Whether your motivation is *away* from a future that under no circumstances do you wish to bring about or whether it's *towards* a future that is so damn amazing and worthwhile that why would you not put every ounce of effort into making it happen - there's something in here for you.

BLAG IT 'TIL YOU BAG IT

When it comes to attracting the success that we desire, there's a lot to be said about the value of pre-supposing success or blagging it 'til you bag it.

By modelling the mindset, thoughts, behaviours and actions of our 'smashed it' self, we send a message out to the universe, but probably most importantly to ourselves, that we are serious about this. So serious, in fact, that come hell or high water, we will achieve it. We will make it happen and with every step we take towards that future, the universe edges it one step closer in our direction.

What would you do if you knew that you had the full and complete backing of the universe?

DON'T KNOW WHERE TO START?

You may find that you have so many things to go after that you don't know where to start. It may be that you've put off making progress in some areas of your life for a while, either because the time wasn't right or there were other things that required your attention. Well, dear Diva, now is the time for you to place the spotlight on your own wants, needs and desires. The first thing to do is to get all those things out of your head and down on paper. The Wheel of Life can help you do just that. It goes like this:

1. Grab yourself a piece of paper and draw a large circle.
2. Divide the circle into however many parts you need to represent each of your goals and aims, then label them. You can have as many as you please; that is a diva's prerogative after all.
3. Imagining that the centre of the wheel is 0 and the outside edge is 10, rate each goal in terms of its relative priority.
4. Step back, take a look and then ask yourself:
   » What am I noticing about my goals?
   » Which are being driven by me (intrinsic) and which are being driven by someone else's agenda (extrinsic)?
   » Which goals are being driven by 'must' 'need' and 'should', as opposed to 'want' 'desire' or 'love to'?
   » Which are interdependent and so if I do one, I also strike off the other?
   » Taking all of that into consideration, where would I like to begin?

You don't need to see the whole staircase to take the first step - Martin Luther King Jr

GOALS THAT MAKE YOU GO 'OOOH'

This is a bloody gorgeous way for you to think about creating goals that, as the title says, make you go *Oooh*. Goals that fulfil you on all sorts of levels. Goals that allow you to do the things that give you energy and that you're good at. Goals that bring you a sense of meaning, connecting you to a higher purpose. And goals that bring you pleasure, that are fun and that you will enjoy. This approach is by Tal-Ben Shahar. Its beauty is in its simplicity:

- What gives me meaning?
- What gives me pleasure?
- What plays to my strengths?

The idea is that by creating goals which intersect at that magic spot in the middle, you will find fulfilment. You might like to ask yourself these questions about a situation in your own life right now as a way of exploring what is going on at a deeper level.

For example, if you were to think about your career right now:

- Does the work give you meaning? Does it connect to your higher purpose/your 'why'?
- Does it give you pleasure? Does it make you happy?
- Does it make the most of your strengths? Does the work leave you energised and feeling good?

If the answer to any of those questions is no, then it's time to look closer at what's going on. By that I don't mean jack it all in and leave your job. But I invite you to think about what it would take for you to bring just a little bit more of each of these into your work right now.

MAKING STUFF HAPPEN

So, you have your goal and you understand your why. You know for whom you are doing it, you know what's driving it (towards or away from) and you've explored your two futures. Here are some handy questions to help guide you as to where you go next:

1. Name it. Take your goal, give it a single sentence description and decide when you want to have achieved it by. For example, *I want to have achieved...by...*

2. Learn from the past. What have you done about it so far? What got in the way of you achieving it last time?

3. Gather your resources. What will you need to get this done?

4. Take your own advice. If somebody you knew was in the same position, what would you tell them to do?

5. Think big. List all the things that you could do to make this thing happen.

6. Plan ahead. What could get in your way? How might you overcome it?

7. Ask for help. What support do you need and who could you call on? Make full use of your entourage.
8. Start somewhere. What one small step could you take to edge you that little bit closer?

TOP TIPS

- Make your goals more intrinsic. *I want to do... because it will benefit me in...*
- Share your goal with somebody. Ask them to check in on your progress. This makes you more accountable for doing the things you say you will
- Take small steps. Don't bite off more than you can chew; otherwise you will set yourself up for failure. Break it down into small, achievable steps with realistic deadlines.
- Expect, but don't assume setbacks. This isn't a Disney fairy tale, things will get in the way. Deal with them as they arise, remember all the times that you overcame similar challenges in the past and keep your eye on the prize.
- Keep an ear out for unhelpful self-talk. Recognise that its intent is to keep you safe. But safe equals small. Let the voice in your head know you've heard it, perhaps even thank it, then do the opposite of what it says.
- Celebrate small wins. Progress is progress, no matter how small. Recognise your successes and give yourself a pat on the back. This helps

to keep you motivated and will sustain you on the next leg.

- Have a successful relationship with the present; don't wait until you've got to where you want to be. Success = everyday behaviours associated with long-term outcomes (blag it 'til you bag it).
- Take care of your mind, body and soul. It's hard work turning your goals into a reality. It takes energy, focus, determination, resilience and tenacity. It also takes a good amount of work on yourself. It requires you to understand yourself: Why do you do the things you do? Why do you want the things you want? How are you getting in your own way? It requires you to manage unhelpful self-talk and to unpick your relationship with failure. The list goes on and on and I'm exhausted just writing about it. Give yourself a break from time to time, cut yourself some slack and take care of yourself.

ADVICE FROM MY HUSBAND

- Avoid making your goals too big or specific. Keep them fluid and be prepared to tweak them along the way as you learn.
- Having dreams and aspirations are good, but don't make your goal 'the dream'. Make your goals the steps you will take to get there.

SECOND MOUNTAIN SYNDROME

If you are driven, if you make it your habit to set your sights on something and achieve it, then it can be easy to misplace your sense of perspective and move too quickly onto the next challenge before having given proper time and consideration to what you've done and how far you've come. Yes, you might want to maintain the momentum you've created, but in doing so, you run the risk of robbing yourself of three key things:

1. The valuable lessons and insights that can serve you well in your next endeavour.
2. The joy to be had in seeing how far you've come and in celebrating your success.
3. Time to stand still, to rest and recover before you go again.

I call this habit 'Second Mountain Syndrome'. You've set a goal for yourself, you've fought through the snow and the ice to reach the top of that mountain, and then before you can even take in the view and look back at how far you've climbed, you've set your sights on a new mountain, and before you've planted your flag - you're off again.

Don't forget to stop, have a glass of fizz and take in the view from the top.

CHAPTER SIX

BLAG IT 'TIL YOU BAG IT

A diva doesn't wait to be successful at some point in the future. A diva has a successful relationship with the present moment.

THE LAW OF ATTRACTION

Whether you think you can or you think you can't, you're right.

Whatever the mind can conceive and believe it can achieve.

Positive energy attracts positive outcomes.

These statements all say the same thing - what you think about determines what you bring about.

Put simply: Thought = Action = Result

Your thoughts determine the actions you take (or don't), which in turn determines your results:

- I think I'm rubbish at singing, so I don't practise and I don't become a professional singer.
- I don't think I'm good enough for the promotion, so I don't put myself forward and I don't get promoted.
- I don't think I'm worthy of love, so I don't put myself out there and I stay single.

Now, it may well be that you are an awful singer, a terrible employee and an even worse partner - but what if you aren't? What if the only thing standing in the way of the things you want in your life is, well, you? To be more specific, how you think. In the examples above, we aren't even talking about grand plans and ideas, we're talking about the basics, right? Having hobbies, a career and finding love. These are entry-level goals, of which you are more than worthy, dear Diva.

Some believe in fate, the idea that our future is defined for us and that we are merely passengers along for the ride. I take a different view. I believe that we create our future, which means that the buck stops with us. When our end inevitably comes and we look back on how we spent our time, if we are dissatisfied with our 'performance', then we only have ourselves to blame. Now to be clear, what I'm not saying here is that we are responsible for the bad stuff that happens *to* us, of course not. However, what we are responsible for is how we deal with the bad stuff and the degree to which we allow it to define us and determine our future actions - and non-actions.

The interesting bit in all this is the part that the unseen forces play, whether that's what some describe as God or the universe or perhaps even our subconscious shepherding us along. Regardless, when we really believe in what we're doing, we can almost always find a way to make it happen. Whilst I believe that we create our futures, I also believe that when we really want it, when we visualise it and put our goals and ambitions out into the world, something happens. If we believe in it enough, if we want it enough, then those forces align with us and gently nudge us along in the right direction.

There are two things to remember when it comes to attracting what we want into our lives.

The first is that just as thoughts attract results, thoughts also determine how we interpret those results and how we interpret success itself. If we become fixated on one ideal version of success and aren't open to other possibilities, then we risk not seeing what is right under our nose. What I mean is, we dream of something, we put in the work to make it happen and opportunities then present. But because these don't fit with the ideal image we have in our heads, the image of what success would be like for us, we allow them to pass us by. So, lesson one - stay present, notice what is going on around you and remain open to success presenting itself in many different forms. What might at first appear to be a distraction, something that isn't worthy of your attention, may just be the very thing you've been working towards, in disguise.

The second is that if we're serious about the change we want to see in our lives, we have to put in the bloody work. It's not a case of ask and it shall be delivered. If it was that easy, I wouldn't need to share this stuff with the world. Change requires effort. It requires you to get out there and hustle. To try stuff out, to meet new people, to take risks. To win some and lose some and to learn along the way.

This metaphor sums up both points perfectly:

You ask the universe for a cake. It delivers you the flour, the eggs, the butter and the sugar. All you have to do is bring them together, but you can't be bothered. So you stay hungry.

BLAG IT 'TIL YOU BAG IT

Psychologists and coaches refer to this as 'pre-supposing success'. I prefer 'blag it 'til you bag it' - it's the same thing.

This approach has served me well over the years and it couldn't be simpler. Essentially, it's about thinking, acting and behaving as if you've already achieved the thing that you want. Don't get me wrong, by this, I don't mean going around telling people in the street that you've just signed a major record deal or opened a fancy restaurant in Mayfair, when in fact you haven't. That's lying, which isn't befitting of a diva. What it is about, however, is modelling the mindset and behaviours of your future self, the future self that has already achieved what you are setting out to do. This elicits a physical and neurological response in your body which you can use to keep you motivated on your quest for success. It starts with visualisation.

Everything is energy and that's all there really is. Match the frequency of the reality you want and you cannot help but get that reality. It can be no other way. This is not philosophy. This is physics - Albert Einstein

VISIONING SUCCESS

Your brain is an amazing thing. But for all its amazingness, it has a few quirks - like all good things. One quirk that we can use to our advantage is that it finds it almost impossible to tell the difference between something that has already happened (a memory) and something that is yet to happen (a dream or vision). If you are interested in the research behind this, just Google 'David R Hamilton Piano Research'. By pre-supposing or visualising success, we can trick our mind and body into thinking we've already achieved the thing we're setting out to. This causes an influx of dopamine, which does two things. It makes us feel good, but more importantly, it helps us to think more broadly and creatively, giving us a helpful route to explore how we made our success happen. Dopamine, the happiness hormone, is the important factor in this, because as the saying goes, 'Nobody ever had a bright idea whilst running away from a lion'.

Once we've spent time visualising our success and really feeling how it feels to have got there, we can then retrace the steps we took and explore how we overcame any obstacles that got in our way. Speaking from a place of having been there, done it and got the t-shirt not only provides us with some clear actions, but more importantly, it gives us the confidence, belief and motivation to get out there and make the damn thing happen. It's then a case of keeping that sense of achievement with us at all times. When we come up against barriers, we recall how good it felt to have achieved it and this motivates us to get our shit together, find a solution and keep moving forward.

The secret to making stuff happen? Believe that it's already yours.

Give it a try, trust me here...it's visceral, it's powerful, it's inspiring - and it goes like this:

STEP 1: Think of the thing you want to achieve - hold it clearly in your mind.

Then think of a point in the future when you want to have achieved it by - keep it realistic.

Now imagine a future version of yourself walking towards you, having achieved all the things you wanted.

Notice them:

- What do they look like? What's their facial expression?
- What clothes are they wearing? What about their shoes? (Shoes are always a giveaway.)
- How do they carry themselves? How do they interact with the world around them?

Really notice what they are like. Spend as much time here as possible.

STEP 2: When you're ready, step into their shoes and feel all their success. Notice any changes in your body: your heart rate, posture, shoulders lowering, etc. Now, speaking from a point of view of having been there and done it, talk back to yourself today:

- How did you make it happen?
- How did you overcome any obstacles?
- Who helped you? Remember, no diva is an island; it takes an entourage!
- What advice will you give your past self?

STEP 3: Now, bring all that success, belief and confidence back to yourself today. What's the one step you will take today/this week to move forward?

Visualise your success, believe it and then prove yourself right. You are the creator of the path you travel, as well as the only obstacle that will ever block its way.

A NOTE ON MANIFESTING

No, I'm not talking about broomsticks and black flame candles - stay with me here. It seems like everyone is talking about manifesting. It's everywhere, from magazines, online, social media and in just about every celebrity book going. If you don't know much about it, then it can appear a lot more complicated than it is. Even the term 'manifesting' makes it sound like something that Bette Midler would do around a cauldron. In truth, it's dead easy. Essentially, manifesting is asking the universe to bring you something that you desire through the laws of attraction (you get back what you put out) and through your own belief that it will happen (think it and it will come). Simply, it is making your goals and dreams a reality through your thoughts, beliefs, actions and reactions.

There are many approaches out there, but typically they all boil down to this:

1. **Know what you want.** You first need to have put the work in to figure out what you want to be different, why you want it and how it will benefit you - see the chapter titled 'Goals'.

2. **Be clear and specific.** The universe doesn't do vague. Rather than saying, *I want a new job*, build up as detailed a picture as you can. The activities that follow will help with this. With this job example, think about the type of work you'd like to be doing, how you want to feel when you wake up and go to bed, the kind of lifestyle you'd like your new job to afford you, what clothes you'd wear or car you'd drive - details matter.

3. **Put it out to the universe.** Once you've pinpointed what you want, you have some choices. You can meditate on it, visualise it, speak it aloud, create a vision board/box or write it down.

4. **Act like it's in the bag.** Start thinking and behaving as if you've already achieved it.

5. **Notice what you get back.** Take time to celebrate small successes and every bit of progress made, even if at first it doesn't seem like progress. For example, applying for a job and not being

successful is still progress! You backed yourself, you put yourself out there, you were brave - nice job.

6. **Trust the process** - Be OK with not knowing what's coming next and try and enjoy the journey.

Note: Don't expect things to happen overnight. This kind of work takes time, patience and repetition - it also requires action on your part.

Nothing works unless you do. Things won't just fall into your lap, you have to be out there playing the field for the opportunities and connections to reveal themselves.

WRITE A LETTER TO YOURSELF / THE UNIVERSE

If visualisation isn't your thing, but words are, then try writing your thoughts down instead. This approach is just as powerful and the act of committing your wants and desires to paper adds a different dimension. Through the act of writing, you are giving life to this thing that you desire - you are taking it out of your head and bringing it into the physical world - *oh hey girl.*

A really nice way of doing this is to write yourself a letter, or if you prefer, write the universe a letter. Here's how it works...

Believe it can be done. When you believe, your mind will find ways to make it happen.

DEAR (NAME/UNIVERSE)

- Write the letter from yourself, using 'I'.
- Write it from the point of view of having achieved what you set out to. *I've done/achieved x...*
- Begin with the date and then describe where you are writing from. *It's January 1st, 20XX and I'm writing to you from my hotel room in New York City...*
- Share the details of your success, what you've achieved, how you achieved it and who helped you along the way.
- Describe what your future self is like, what you enjoy doing, how you spend your day, what you do to relax, etc.
- There is no right or wrong way. Go with your gut and try not to overthink it. Be ambitious but keep it realistic.
- Sign your letter and put it somewhere special, perhaps by your bed. You could even give it to a friend for safekeeping and ask that they give it back to you on a meaningful date in the future or write it as an email and schedule it to be sent on a date you specify.
- The final step? Get to work.

Credit: Barefoot Coaching

CREATE A VISION BOARD / BOX

Create a vision board or box of items that represent the thing that you want to achieve.

For example, if you want to start a cupcake business, you might include things like:

- The recipes you'd use.
- Photographs of cakes you'd bake.
- Your company logo or branding.
- A picture of a van with your logo on it.
- An imaginary five-star customer review.
- An apron or other clothing that you'd wear to work.
- Post-it notes with thoughts or emotions that you'd think or feel as you go about your work each day, e.g. *free, creative, my own boss, no rules, using my strengths, loving life,* etc. Now I want to start a cupcake business!

There really are no rules. Give it a go. During the process of writing this book, I created a vision board which included a mock-up of its front cover. Whenever I questioned whether I'd get there and finish it, or when I was exhausted and needed a boost, I'd look at it and think about how good I'd feel when that first edition arrived on my doorstep. I'd then think about how amazing it would be to share it with the world and with my friends and family at my very own book launch.

Right now, I'm about halfway through writing it and I've already planned the guest list and the venue for the launch! Not only is this giving me the motivation to make sure that I finish it by the deadline, but 'blagging it 'til I bag it' offers me the belief and motivation needed to get it done.

What will your vision board or box look like?

WRITE YOUR VERY OWN DIVA FEATURE

What diva wouldn't want to appear in print? Well, now is your chance. You can come at this from a few different angles. You can write about yourself having achieved the things that you want to, which is another way of motivating yourself towards success - especially if you pin it to your office wall or stick it to your fridge. Or you can write it purely about the characteristics which make you utterly fabulous - in that sense, I suppose it becomes more of a character reference, something to look back on whenever you need a confidence boost. Written from this position, it makes a gorgeous gift for somebody in your life who needs to remember their brilliance - write them their own DIVA Feature, frame it and give it to them as a gift.

Tip: Whichever angle you take and whomever you write about, know that modesty has no place here. The whole point is to sell the person you are writing about, big them up and accentuate all their best features.

Here's how it works:

- Imagine you are being interviewed by a reporter from the most luxurious and expensive magazine in town. They are going to write about you, your experiences, your career history, your purpose and the work you do. They are going to present you in the best possible light, seeing the very best of you but not straying from the truth.
- Write the article which they would write about you. Don't overthink or over-edit it. Put yourself in the imaginary reporter's shoes, ignore any 'oh no, I can't write that' or 'that's going too far now' - showcase yourself at your very best.

Pin it up somewhere or give it to somebody as a gift!

Credit: Barefoot Coaching

The way we talk to ourselves is important because it becomes the basis of our spoken word. It sets up the mental atmosphere that we operate in, and that attracts to us experiences.
- Louise Hay

SYNCHRONICITY

Synchronicity is a term originally coined by psychologist Carl Jung that refers to deeply meaningful coincidences which occur in your life. For example, as I was grappling with writing this book, I recalled one day that my grandmother had particularly liked a song that had the line 'follow that rainbow and your dreams will all come true'. I too had loved this song growing up without really knowing why; the words didn't hold any meaning for me as a kid. I thought about her and that song a lot throughout the early stages of writing. Then I noticed something that at first, I admit, freaked me out. It appeared that whenever I was doubting myself, feeling as though I couldn't do it, feeling exhausted and thinking of giving up - that song would come on the radio. I'd get in the car and there it would be. I'd walk into a shop and there it would be. An advert would come on the TV and there it would be. And on the days when I'd shut myself away from distraction, I'd look out of my window and there it would be - in the form of an actual rainbow. The more I acknowledged these synchronicities aloud, *OK, I get it - keep on moving, don't give up*, the more they appeared, always at the perfect time. Now I'm no expert on the topic or the psychology/ mystery behind the concept of synchronicity. What I do know is that I've experienced the profound power of deeply meaningful synchronicities in my life that I found personally helpful. They kept me going. They left me feeling like I was on the right path and that I wasn't alone. They gave me confidence that it would all be worth it. Spiritual phenomena? Psychological phenomena? Or something else? If they help, if they're comforting - who cares?

As you do this work, notice synchronicities appearing where they didn't before. Either because you weren't looking, you weren't open to them or because you were working against yourself, rather than with yourself. By this, I mean that you were acting or behaving in a way that wasn't in alignment with who you really are and what you really care about. It's a bit like trying to force yourself into a shoe that you knew didn't fit, but you tried anyway.

My belief is that when we begin to work in alignment with ourselves, our identity, values, beliefs and strengths, the universe begins to move with us, rather than against us. I like to think of it as the universe gently (although not always) nudging people, opportunities, realisations, new thoughts and understanding in our direction. There are many definitions of synchronicity, here are just a few that resonate with me personally:

A meaningful coincidence of two or more events where something other than the probability of chance is involved - Carl Jung

A 'meaningful coincidence' of outer and inner events that are not themselves causally connected. The emphasis lies on the word meaningful - Marie-Louise von Franz

An inexplicable and profoundly meaningful coincidence that stirs the soul and offers a glimpse of one's destiny - Phil Cousineau

I like to think of synchronicities as random 'happenings' that connect my thoughts, dreams or goals (internal) to the physical world (external). Synchronicities are events which coincide with the thought process rather than originating from it.

If you find yourself experiencing spooky or too good to be true coincidences that repeat, rather than a single experience of good fortune, then you may well be experiencing the power of synchronicity. Acknowledge them and share your thanks out loud because this, dear Diva, is the universe's way of letting you know that you're on the right track. Crack on.

Examples of Synchronicity:

- You think about a friend you haven't talked to in years and suddenly receive a phone call or message from them.

- You have a dream about a specific event or person and then that event or person appears in your life soon after.
- You have a deep feeling that you should go to a certain place at a certain time and when you do, you meet someone who changes your life.
- You are reading a book and the information or message in the book is exactly what you needed to hear at that moment.
- You think of a solution to a problem that has been bothering you for a while and then you hear or read about that same solution shortly after.

Synchronicity is the universe's way of saying 'yes'.

DO THE BLOODY WORK

The 'blag it 'til you bag it' approach can prove to be immensely rewarding. But it's not a case of 'imagine it and it will come'. Unless you've developed a knack for Jedi mind control, you have to put in the work for things to start to work. Having a positive, successful, abundant mindset is a brilliant way to get started; it's half the battle, maybe even more than half for some of us. But nothing will work unless you do. Don't know where to start? Start somewhere. A bit like how I imagine being an actor is, you can have all the talent and skill in the world and be the best at what you do, but if nobody sees you, if you aren't noticed, well then you aren't going anywhere. Even the best actors had to start somewhere, taking jobs they didn't really want to take, making mistakes and learning from them, each job an opportunity to get noticed by the right people, to be seen in the right places, by the right people at the right time. To switch up the analogy, you have to be out there playing the field, shoot some, miss some and score some until the universe has no option but to take notice and say, *OK, I see you. I see how much you want this and I also see that you're willing to put in the graft to make it happen. Here's a little nudge in the right direction courtesy of old momma universe.* Yes, I gendered the universe.

Do yourself and all those who came before you a favour and do the bloody work.

DON'T LET MENTAL MASTURBATION SEND YOU BLIND

No, I haven't lost my mind; hear me out. Mental Masturbation is where you 'get off' on thinking and talking about the thing you are going to do without getting on and doing it. Each time you dream about writing that book, moving to Spain or running a little B&B or bookshop, you flood your brain with the chemical dopamine, which gives the sensation of a positive high. When met with the positive reactions of people you talk to about your goals, for example, *Oh my gosh, you are amazing, I wish I could do that,* you only deepen and extend the high. Now, I'm a big fan of telling people about my goals (the ones I'm serious about) because it helps keep me committed to achieving them. When I wobble, the people I've told remind me of why I wanted to get started in the first place and they give me a kick start to get going again. When I'm not making the progress I'd like to or said I would, those same people hold me accountable by saying, *Right, when are you going to do this by then, hmm?* But, as with many things in life, it is possible to have too much of a good thing. Talking about what you want to do, without taking action to move it on, can lead to a vicious cycle:

- You decide you're going to do something.
- You tell people about it.
- You feel the kick of the dopamine high.

- You take little to no action.
- You repeat the kick when you want to feel good.

Avoid falling into this trap. You are edging yourself on knowing full well that there is little to no chance of climax.

Don't be a jerk - if you say you're going to do it, bloody well do it, or sack it off. I said 'sack'.

FOCUS ON THE PROCESS, NOT THE PRODUCT

This might seem counter-intuitive, seeing as we've spent this chapter visualising what it is we want and what it will be like to get there. But there's a balance to be found. You want it and you believe you are capable and worthy of getting it - great. But don't allow yourself to be so absorbed in the future that you miss out on the present. After all, the steps you take today, in this moment, the places you go, the people you meet and the opportunities that open up today, are what create your tomorrow. A bit like a 3D printer laying one layer on top of the other, slowly and consistently, until everything comes together and the final construction makes sense. Visualising the future is not about living in a dream world. It's about taking inspiration and valuable motivation from the future to help us in the present. The present is all we ever have, dear Diva, and so if we live our lives in the future - we are hallucinating. Take that valuable insight, wisdom and motivation and put it to work in the here and now. Use it to edge you closer to what it is you want in your life, but be careful to not allow it to consume you. What's more, enjoy it - you will never get this time again. If you want this thing badly enough, then you will make it happen. So why not spend this time really enjoying the journey? Set your sights, do the work and then enjoy the experience. There will be so much in your current life that you have already brought about; don't disregard what you have in the here and now by obsessing about what's to come. Strike a balance and then jump in and enjoy the ride.

> *Don't wait to be successful at some future point. Have a successful relationship with the present moment and be fully present in whatever you are doing. That is success.*
> *- Eckhart Tolle*

PATIENCE, DEAR DIVA

Timing is everything. Think about the most successful events in your life so far - jobs, achievements, relationships, kids, etc. Could they have happened ten years before? How about five? If they had, how might they have been different? Would you have wanted them to be different? If the job was different, your partner and kids were different? Would the opportunity have even been there? Would you have even been ready to notice it, let alone take it? A place for everything and everything in its place, dear Diva. If you want it badly enough and you put in the work to get there, then the chances are it will come. If you were handed the thing you want tomorrow with no questions asked, there it is; take it. Would you be ready to receive it? Stop and really think about that. Put any ego to one side and sit with the question for a moment. If you aren't sure, if there's more work you need to do, either practically or emotionally, then there's your answer. For you to be able to receive it without it blowing up in your face, you have to be ready. If you aren't - get ready. But worry not, dear Diva, because you aren't going at this alone. As well as your wonderful entourage of friends, family and connections, you've got little old me. Let's make shit happen.

When destiny knocks, you better be ready. Because if you aren't, you won't even hear the knock.

CHAPTER SEVEN

GETTING SHIT DONE

A diva knows that the best way to predict the future is to create it.

DECISION MAKING

In the day-to-day life of a diva, there are decisions to be made left, right and centre. Most you will make without too much thought: what to wear, what to have for breakfast or which way to ask your driver to take you to work. There will be some decisions, however, which require more careful consideration. Ones perhaps in which the stakes are seemingly high.

I'm blessed to be surrounded by many strong women. Women who know their minds and are clear on what it is they want, be it from life, from love or from their work. But on occasion, even these divas stumble when it comes to some decisions, particularly those with the potential to impact those around them. If you are of a kind and compassionate nature, it's only normal to be concerned about the welfare of others and how your actions may or may not impact those you love and care for. The challenge comes when the self-talk creeps in, the catastrophic thinking, *If I take this job, then I won't be back in time for dinner, my children won't ever see me, they'll forget who I am, I won't be a mum anymore.* The 'all or nothingness', *If I do this, then I have to say goodbye to my entire social life; I'll never be able to go out again.* Or those prone to more informed decision making, over heart and gut, may experience 'analysis paralysis', a state where you are so consumed with the details, the options and the fear of making the 'wrong' choice, that you are paralysed with fear.

Even when presented with the most out of this world no-brainer opportunity, the most self-assured diva can find themselves at an impasse - and that can be especially hard if you are used to knowing what you want.

HEAD - HEART - GUT

One way to help find a way through is to check in with all three of your decision making centres - your head, your heart and your gut. Most of us tend to rely on one, maybe two of these centres to help steer and guide us. But it can be helpful to tune in to all three. It might just provide you with the helpful insight that you need to move forward.

Head (I Think): Your head centre deals in logic, facts, reasoning and plans. This is where you look at pros and cons, make lists, weigh up benefits and risks and explore, practically, whether saying yes is worth it. Your head centre might sound like, *It would make sense to...* or *I should/shouldn't...*

Heart (I Feel): Your heart centre deals with feelings, emotions, visions and dreams. In your heart, there are no rules, no practicalities. This is about what you want and desire and how you can get there as quickly and as easily as possible. Your heart centre might sound like, *I must...* or *I need/want...*

Gut (My Intuition Tells Me): Your gut centre deals with instinct, intuition and immediate responses. It doesn't deal with desires or facts; in fact, it defies reason altogether. The gut centre is about a sense of feeling, *This feels right/wrong* and *I just have this hunch that...* While you might not be able to put your finger on why your gut is leaning one way or another, it's an important barometer to take note of.

Tapping into all three centres when making a decision means that you will be much more likely to enter into that decision confidently and in alignment with yourself, making you much more likely to see it through. Making a decision based only on logic and reasoning alone, whilst it might make sense, could lead to you missing out personally in some way, either in the fun department or in terms of your own dreams and goals. On the other hand, making decisions based solely on what your heart tells you, whilst it might be fun and in the interests of your broader goals and desires, might be impractical in all sorts of ways. And then there's the gut. To make decisions based solely on your gut response, whilst it might be liberating to be a completely free spirit attuned to yourself and Mother Earth, might lead to all sorts of consequences.

The best way to avoid internal conflicts around your decision making is to tap into all three.

So, next time you're faced with a decision, even a straightforward one, ask yourself:

- What is my head telling me?
- What is my heart telling me?
- What is my gut telling me?

THE YES / NO APPROACH

If like me, you find tapping into your head centre a bit more challenging, then here's another quick and easy way of approaching a decision. It's a bit like a pros and cons list but for people like me who don't deal well with too much detail. It goes like this:

If I were to say *yes* to this, what would I be saying *no* to?

And vice versa:

If I were to say *no* to this, what would I be saying *yes* to?

I used this recently with a darling friend of mine who was offered a job and was struggling with what to do. Her heart was telling her something different to her head and her gut was all over the place. We explored together and she said, 'Well, if I say yes to this job, then I'd be saying no to working for myself, no to going on holiday whenever I like and no to being free to do the work I want, when I want. On the other hand, I'd also be saying no to worrying about where the money is coming from, no to having to sort out my taxes and accounts and no to feeling like I can't take a holiday because I wouldn't be earning. If I say no to the job, then I'd be saying yes to more time at home, but also, I'd be saying yes to getting serious about running my business.'

If you're wondering what she ended up doing, she took the job.

Give it a go.

When I'm caught between two evils, I like to take the one I've never tried - Mae West

DECISION FLOW

If you really want to go the whole hog, then here's a handy decision flow to guide you to any decision that so crosses your path, dear Diva. You can answer aloud, or you might like to make notes - whichever works for you.

1. What's the decision you are grappling with?
2. When it comes down to it, what is this really about?
3. How much do you want it? And how much is being driven by other people?
4. Why do you want it? What will you gain?
5. Are there any good reasons to do absolutely nothing at all and carry on as you are? Sometimes the most straightforward solution is to do nothing.

6. By saying *yes* to this decision, what will you be saying *no* to?
7. By saying *no* to this decision, what will you be saying *yes* to?
8. If your best friend was in this same situation, what advice would you give them?
9. How might saying yes or no impact on those around you? Your loved ones, family and friends?
10. If you say *yes/no*, what help and support will you need?

Look closely at the present you are constructing; it should look like the future you are dreaming of - Alice Walker

I SMELL A RAT

If your gut tells you that something is up, listen! If you ever find yourself in a position where your gut is telling you that something is off and you're feeling uneasy about a course of action, try checking in with your personal values. These are the things that you stand for (you can read about these in the chapter titled 'Standing Up For Yourself'). For example, you might stand for kindness, compassion and openness, but you may find yourself in a position where you are asked to act in a way that conflicts with the fundamental beliefs you hold about what is the right and proper way to do things. Here are two questions to keep in your back pocket when you find yourself in this position:

1. How comfortably does this situation sit with your values and what you believe in?
2. What would happen to the world if everybody did it?

I bloody love that last one.

PRIORITISATION

I get it; you're a busy bitch. You've got places to go, people to see and stuff to do. But try as you might, you can't do it all - unless you're fortunate enough to have a team of people around you to hand off to. It comes down to you, dear Diva. And if you are going to stay healthy and have time for yourself, you will need to decide what you will do now and what you will leave until later - or even better, sack off altogether. It's hard, I know, but you can't do it all. If you find yourself with too much on your plate and you aren't sure of what needs to give, take a closer look at that plate:

1. Imagine a plate in front of you.
2. Divide the plate into however many portions you need to represent each of the things you have going on right now.
3. Imagining that the centre of the plate is 0 and the outside rim is 10, rate each portion in terms of its relative priority.

4. Step back and take a look, then ask yourself:
   - » What am I noticing about what I've got going on?
   - » How much of my time is being given to other people's agendas rather than my own?
   - » Which are interdependent and so if I tick off one, I also tick off the other?
   - » Which are important and which are urgent? (There's a big difference.)
   - » Which do I need to do something about today and which can wait?

BIG DIAMOND OR LITTLE GEM?

I like this concept. It has its roots in the business world, where the priorities for the year are sometimes referred to as 'Big Rocks' (I know). I've given it a much needed upgrade and the rocks have now become diamonds - much better. The concept is the same, you have:

Big Diamonds: Your main goals and priorities, the things you want to achieve in life.

Little Gems: These are still important to your daily living but don't contribute directly to your Big Diamonds.

Glitter: This is all of the small stuff that comes at you each day and gets in the way.

Now, imagine that you were given a jar and to this jar, you added your glitter. So much glitter in fact, that there wasn't enough room for your Little Gems, never mind your Big Diamonds.

You're full! But fear not, we're going again.

This time you start by adding your Big Diamonds (your big priorities). Even though the jar is pretty full, you go ahead and add your Little Gems (dull but necessary stuff). With a little shake, they find their way into the gaps between the Big Diamonds and they settle nicely. The jar is still looking full, but you go ahead and pour in your Glitter. With another shake, the glitter fills any remaining space and the jar is full.

The learning here is to focus your time and energy on your Big Diamonds first, whatever they might be - your health, spending more time with your family, writing a book! Then and only then, add in the rest.

When you find that you're going from place to place, meeting to meeting, picking up task after task and you're struggling to know what to give your attention to first, ask yourself...

Is this a big diamond, a little gem or are we just dealing with glitter here? In which case, blow that shit away - it gets everywhere.

ASK FOR HELP

During periods of stress, strain or overwhelm, when we feel like our back is against the wall, we can lose sight of three things:

First, our sense of perspective. We become focused on the task or challenge at hand and lose sight of the bigger picture. This can make the situation seem much worse than it actually is. Make a conscious choice to step outside of yourself for a moment, to see yourself from outside of yourself and to ask:

- What's actually going on here?
- How big a deal is this really?

And one of my favourite questions:

- What's the simplest and most stress-free option for me here?

This can be just what is needed to flip a switch and help you think more broadly and creatively about what you've got going on. Check out the chapter titled 'Worrying' if you want to explore some tools and strategies for regaining your sense of perspective.

Second, we lose sight of who the heck we are. Our minds are so focused on the present, that we forget about all the times in the past when we tried and we succeeded. Where we faced challenges or difficult times and we got through it in one piece. This learning is invaluable when it comes to helping us in the here and now. Ask yourself:

- When have I faced something like this before?
- What did that experience teach me?
- How could I use some of that to help me in the present?

Finally, and most importantly, we forget that we don't have to do it all by ourselves. Humans are not meant to exist alone; we aren't designed for it, psychologically, emotionally and physically. We wouldn't even be here if that were true. You are surrounded by people who love and care for you, who would be willing to do whatever was needed to help you out if you were in a pickle and I've no doubt you'd be saying the same if the stiletto were on the other foot. Don't let pride, embarrassment, fear or feeling like you're being a burden stand in the way of asking for what you need. If you do, not only are you giving in to your ego, but you are robbing yourself of the joy that comes with receiving kindness.

Ask yourself:

- Who could help me?
- Who do I know who has faced something similar before?
- What might I be able to offer them in return?

THE THREE BITCHES OF THE APOCALYPSE

We are going to end this chapter with three words that I honestly believe are amongst the most damaging and limiting words a person can say to themselves, yet these silent assassins bob along merrily until they infiltrate our daily lives and kick up a storm. What words could be so dreadful as to cause that sort of damage, you ask? These:

- Must.
- Should.
- Need.

They sound all innocent at first, *Oh, I must put the washing on before I...* or *I should really have 'so and so' for Christmas.*

The thing that each of these words has in common is that they indicate a motivation that is coming from somewhere other than ourselves. I don't *want* to do it, but I feel that I *must/need/should.* If unchecked, a person can find themselves going about their life focusing on everything other than the things that they actually want and desire, things that might bring them joy and meaning. That sends a message that your own needs are not as important as those of others.

I've made it my business now to speak up anytime I hear somebody say one of these three words. I reply with, 'Need to? According to who?' Or 'What would happen if you didn't? What could you spend your time doing instead?'

I end here because the language we use is important. A belief is nothing more than a thought repeated. When we are juggling busy lives and balancing lots of different things, it's easy to let our focus slip and begin to tell ourselves that the small stuff is more important than the big stuff.

Give it a go. Over the next 24 hours, take notice of the seemingly innocent truths you tell yourself about what's important and what isn't. Notice the *musts*, *shoulds* and the *needs* and then ask yourself:

- Is that true? According to whom?
- What's the worst that would happen if I didn't do it?
- What could I be spending my valuable time and energy doing instead?

Don't waste any more of your precious time musterbating.

—CHAPTER EIGHT—

FAILURE

A diva knows that failure is merely success in progress.

'FAILURE'

I'm starting this chapter with some sound advice from a dear friend...

'Always look amazing. That way, regardless of what happens, people will say, *Damn, they look shit hot.*'

Perhaps you have noticed the quotation marks around the word 'Failure'? That, dear Diva, is because in the mind of a diva, failure is an illusion. It exists only in the mind and is nothing more than our way of saying that something didn't go the way we'd expected it to. The Dali Lama is quoted as saying...

I never fail. I either win, or I learn.

Adopting the mindset that failure is an illusion cooked up for us by society can be incredibly freeing. You can cast off the idea that if you give something a go and it doesn't work out, you haven't failed, you've learned and you will come back next time, armed with that learning, that knowledge and that insight and you will go again.

What failure really boils down to is the expectations that you place on yourself. The idea that you have one chance and one chance only to get things right and if things don't go to plan, then you've failed; you are 'a failure'. But you don't stop there. You then self-flagellate by allowing this one episode to define you, attaching all sorts of untruths to yourself, e.g. *I'll never make it work. I'm not good/clever enough. I shouldn't have even tried. I'm not worthy of this anyway. I'll just go back to what I know.*

Bullshit. I'll say it again, failure is a construct. Whether you buy into it or not is down to one person, YOU. You can take the growth mindset approach and put it down to learning, or you can take the fixed mindset approach and wallow in self-pity. If you choose the latter, know that a) this behaviour is not befitting of a diva, and b) you won't be much fun to be around, and nobody likes a misery tits. Instead, say to yourself, *Well that didn't go how I'd expected.* Then dust yourself off, stand up straight, fix your lippy and go again.

NEGATIVE ENERGY ATTRACTS NEGATIVE OUTCOMES

It's true that where your attention goes, grows. Meaning that if you allow yourself to ruminate on failure and put that negative energy out to the world, you are doing the exact opposite of pre-supposing success; you are pre-supposing your failure. If you tell yourself you're going to fail enough, you start to believe it. You then start to think and act in a way which is complicit with the idea of failure and then... you know what happens - you end up taking the lead role in what becomes a shit-fest of a self-fulfilling prophecy.

Ultimately the fight for success is a battle with yourself. Imagine what you could achieve if you joined forces.

FEAR OF FAILURE

It's perfectly normal to fear failure. In fact, it's estimated that almost half of us would say that fear of failure is the biggest roadblock to achieving our goals. Remember what we talked about in the chapter on 'Confidence'? Your brain is designed to protect you, to keep you safe from perceived dangers and threats to your life. But most of the time, we aren't dealing with life and death. What's the worst that could possibly happen if you were to give something a go and it didn't work out? Death? Hardly.

It can be helpful to acknowledge the signals that your brain and body are giving you. I'll often say something to myself like, *OK I hear you, but we're alright. This isn't life and death. You can pipe down and let me enjoy this moment.* It's a bit like having a noisy toddler at your heels seeking attention; once you acknowledge them and let them say their piece, they're happy to go off and leave you alone for a bit. The same is true when it comes to the messages your body sends you.

Better an 'oops' than a 'what if'

FEAR OF EMBARRASSMENT

Having experienced many situations in my life that my critics could argue were failures - catastrophic failures in fact; personal failures, professional failures, relationship failures and career failures, I feel qualified to say that much of that fear of failure comes from the concern that other people will think we have failed. We may worry that they might think about us differently, that they might say unkind things, they might laugh, they may gossip and bitch. Here's my take on that:

1. What other people think of you is none of your damn business - let it go.
2. Most people are far too wrapped up in their own shit to even notice what's going on for you.
3. People will talk, they always have and they always will. You might as well give them something juicy to get their teeth into - I often say that all publicity is good publicity.
4. Accept that if you are going to put yourself out there, you open yourself up to criticism. Aristotle said, 'The only way to avoid criticism is to do nothing, say nothing and be nothing'. That doesn't really go with our outfit, does it, dear Diva?
5. Most people wish they had the guts to do what you are doing. They don't. Instead, they'd rather sit and bitch from the sidelines - let them. That has everything to do with them and absolutely nothing to do with you.

6. The more successful you get, the more public your failures will become. The stakes are higher, you're more visible and there's more pressure to get it right. If you accept that it comes with the territory and try to get a bit more comfortable with it now, you'll thank yourself further down the line.

7. Finally, you owe it to yourself to at least try. Again, better an *oops* than a *what if*.

It's the best fruit that the birds pick at.
- Bette Davis

THE POWER OF 'YET'

'Yet' is a wonderful world. It may be small, but boy is it mighty. It has the power to totally change the story that we tell ourselves. We've already talked about a belief being nothing more than a thought repeated, and so the more we tell ourselves certain 'stories', the more we begin to believe them and then take action or non-action in support of them. When you notice that you're telling yourself a story - an untruth, try adding 'yet' to the end and see what difference it makes.

- I'm no good at singing, yet.
- I can't run 5k, yet.
- I'm not confident enough to give that presentation, yet.
- I'm not qualified enough for that job, yet.

You get the idea.

Mistakes are proof that you're trying.

FAILING FORWARD

I came across this term recently and it's stuck with me. It's a really clear metaphor and I like the image of setbacks propelling you forward, rather than backward. Really, this is all about drawing learning from the times when things didn't go as we'd planned and using that to our advantage in a way that propels us forward - to keep going.

Be brave enough to suck at something new.

FAMOUS 'FAILURES'

I got thinking about the stories of 'famous failures' and how they took that learning, dusted themselves off and came back stronger. Here are just a few well-known faces who have walked this path and come out the other end stronger:

- The greatest basketball player of all time, Michael Jordan, was cut from his high school basketball team.
- Early in his career, Walt Disney was fired from his job at a newspaper because they said he

lacked imagination and had no good ideas.

- Steven Spielberg was rejected from film school three times.
- Albert Einstein was labelled 'mentally slow' on his permanent school record.
- Henry Ford's first two automobile companies failed.
- Oprah Winfrey was fired from an early job as a TV news anchor after being told she was 'unfit for television'.
- Sir James Dyson went through 5,126 failed prototypes before landing on the first working Dyson vacuum.
- Bill Gates dropped out of Harvard and co-owned a business which failed before he started Microsoft.

The universe tests you the most right before you make a breakthrough – it has to make sure that you want it enough.

REDIRECTION

What if the 'failure' you experienced wasn't failure? What if it had nothing to do with what you did or didn't do, with how much you did or didn't know or with what you might have done right and wrong? What if beneath the surface of it all, there was more going on? What if:

- It wasn't the right thing to be doing to start with.
- Had it succeeded, it would have somehow led to pain or suffering.
- Your heart wasn't really in it and deep down you knew it.
- Someone or something was telling you, *Come and play over here...* instead.
- The universe has bigger, brighter and bolder plans for you.

Rejection is divine protection.

QUITTING IS FOR WINNERS

Some of the best decisions I've made in my life have involved throwing in the towel and bowing out. Whether it's been with people or places I've worked, I can hand-on-heart say that whilst others might have looked upon the situation from afar as quitting, those have been amongst the best decisions I've ever made and in most cases, ultimately the most beneficial for me - emotionally, spiritually and financially! There is something very adult-like about knowing when it's time to leave a person, place or situation that is no longer working for you. Learning to walk away and to move on is something that I believe most people would benefit from in some area of their lives. When I think about some of the most successful people I know, people who have built big businesses and achieved high societal status, a 'walking away story' has been key to their success. Quitting does not make you a failure, because success is not defined by 'one shot'. If you believe in what you are doing and it makes you happy then go for it and keep on going until you find a way to make it work. Yes, you might experience a few false starts and redirections, but if you really want it - go for it. And (not but), when the situation stops bringing you joy, when it stops working for you, when the environment begins to hinder, rather than help you, or indeed when you simply change your mind about what you want from your life - walk away and start anew.

This time you aren't starting from scratch, you're starting from experience.

IT'S ONLY A FAILURE IF YOU DON'T LEARN FROM IT

- What are some of the best failures you've experienced in your life?
- What did they teach you?
- In what way were you able to come back stronger?

Looking back on these situations, what would you have changed? Anything?

Every landing is a success if you can walk away from it.

When you wobble (which you will) use your entourage to keep you motivated and focused. They are your biggest cheerleaders.

CHAPTER NINE

CAREER

A diva treats their career like their business, and they manage it like they're the CEO.

'YOU BETTER WERK, BITCH' - RUPAUL

It's estimated that the average person will spend around 90,000 hours at work over their lifetime. Of course, If you love what you do then that's no problem at all. It's hardly work, is it? More an extension of home, a change of scenery - it just so happens that you get paid. Here's the thing, dear Diva, most people go to their place of work, leave their beloved pets/ children in somebody else's care, return depleted and irritated in the dark, do that five times over each week, take the cheque at the end of the month and consider that a fair exchange - well it's not. If you've strayed into that way of thinking, then this chapter is for you. Here's what you need to know. Listen up:

- Your time on this Earth is limited; it's precious - and so are you.
- You deserve to spend your time here doing things that you love, things that energise you and leave you feeling good.
- When you do work like this you start to work in alignment with who you really are and what matters to you.
- You raise your vibration, you put out a different kind of energy and people will notice the difference in you.
- The universe hears the call that you are sending out, *I'm here and ready to do my thing*. It sees you as you are, as who you are becoming and as who you are meant to be - and it responds to your vibration, *I've got you, boo*.

218

YOU ARE NOBODY'S BITCH

You are a walking miracle, dear Diva. You are made of stardust that is billions of years old. Stardust that has had an incomprehensible number of manifestations over its lifetime, constantly reacting to its surroundings and changing, changing again and again until the conditions are just right, and everything is lined up perfectly and then BAM - you appeared. The fact that you are here, reading these words, having this experience, in the skin you are in is a goddamn miracle. You are one of eight billion people on this planet, in an infinite universe in which this Earth is less than a pinprick.

My wish for you, dear Diva, is for you to be happy. For you to understand how special you are, for you to realise your worth and importance and for you to spend your time with people and in places that constantly remind you of that. When it comes to living like a diva, practicalities aside, you can and should have it all. OK, scratch that, you will always have to deal with shitty things, shitty situations, and shitty people, so if we're being real - you can have most of it, most of the time - and that's pretty good in my book. You have a choice. You can put up with work that is:

- Draining your energy.
- Lowering your vibration.
- Keeping you small.
- Wasting your damn time.

Or you can choose to take the path of the diva and say:

Thank you. Thank you for everything you've taught me, for all the people I've met, for all that this job has given me - but It's time for me to do something different now, something that makes me feel more like me.

The moment you start to wonder whether you deserve better - you do.

HIGH-VIBE QUIZ

It might be that you are quite happy with the terms of your 'work exchange' and you've no problem doing what you must in order to get that cheque. Regardless, my hope for you is that you are in a good place surrounded by good people who appreciate and value you and encourage you to be the best, most authentic version of yourself. Take the high-vibe quiz to see how work is working out for you.

Rate each statement on a scale of high, medium or low, based on its relative importance to you.

It's important for me to do work / work for a company that...	H	M	L
Plays to my strengths and leaves me feeling energised			
Brings me joy			
Means I can work independently			
Feels like it's serving a greater purpose (e.g. doing good in the world)			
Allows me to progress and move up the career ladder			
Invests in my training and development			
Allows me to express who I am through the clothes that I wear and my physical appearance			
Respects how I identify and the pronouns I use			
Affords me a healthy work/life balance			
Allows me to take vacation/annual leave without feeling guilty about it			
Allows me to take on more responsibility should I wish (e.g. leading a team)			
Appreciates me for who I am and the skills and talents I bring			
Encourages me to do things in my own way, rather than following set rules and procedures			

Encourages me to speak up and share my point of view			
Allows me to work flexibly around my family and other commitments			
Encourages me to take care of my mental and physical wellbeing			
Allows me to pursue my interests and projects outside of work, should I wish			
Trusts me to make the decisions relating to the work I'm doing			
Sees the benefits of me working from a location of my choosing			
Makes me feel good about myself			
Recognises me for work well done			

Looking back over your ratings:

- What do you notice about your work-based preferences?
- How does the work you're doing now compare?
- How much do you want to do something about it?

You get one go at life, dear Diva. When it comes to how you earn your keep - don't settle for anything less than the best.

Your 9-5 job is someone else's passive income.

TAKE A PEEK BEHIND THE CURTAIN

Have you ever wondered why some people just seem to get on at work without having to put in the work? Have you ever been surprised by who missed out on the promotion and who ended up getting it? Mmhm, I know I have. Ever wondered why some people are always being talked about in meetings even when they aren't there? There have been hundreds of books written about this topic and there are many takes on what it takes to get ahead at work. Here's one. According to Harvey Coleman, 'Empowering Yourself: The Organisational Game Revealed', the secret recipe for success is based on three elements:

Performance: What you do and how well you do it.

Image: What people think of you and how they experience you - what some describe as your 'personal brand'.

Exposure: Who notices you.

You'd be forgiven for assuming that when it comes to work, the thing that bears the most significance in determining whether you get on or not, would be your performance - what you actually do and how well you do it. Surely that's the thing? If you're rubbish at your job then nobody is going to promote you, right? Well, perhaps not. The thing is, you can be the best at what you do, but if nobody knows you're doing it, then when it comes to recognition, pay raise or promotion time, well, you're going to get looked over. It's a harsh reality, but I've got to say from my own time in a big business, it's true. Harvey Coleman says that when it comes to success, performance has very little to do with whether you succeed or not. Doing your job well only gets you 10% of the way there. It's much more about the image that you portray and who notices you. The 'PIE' looks like this:

Performance (10%): The 'What'.

- How skilled and proficient you are at your job.
- The quality of the results that you produce.

Image (30%): The 'How'.

- What people think of you.
- How generally supportive and helpful are you? Are you there when people need you? Are you willing to step in and support when required, go the 'extra mile' and stay late to get the job done?
- How do you show that you take what you do seriously? Are you sharing new ideas and ways of doing things? Do you show that you are interested in your work/company and that you want to learn and grow?
- How do you deal with problems and concerns - do you moan, or do you offer solutions? Do

you look for the negative or accentuate the positive?
- Do you make your boss's life and their boss's life easier by saying, 'Let me handle that for you'?

Exposure 60%: The 'Who'.

- Who knows about you and what you do?
- Does your boss know what you do and how well you do it? Does their boss know? What about their boss?
- Do you allow someone else to step in and represent your work on your behalf? Or do you show up to meetings and represent it yourself? When did you last present something to the management team yourself?
- Do you stop people in the hall and introduce yourself?
- Do you network and collaborate with people outside of your immediate team? Do you network outside of your business? Do you have an online/social media 'presence'?
- Do you get involved in projects, initiatives or extracurricular activities that offer you the opportunity to get noticed? Do you stand up in departmental/company meetings and share what you're working on?
- Do you make yourself visible? Or do you hide your light under a bushel?

The model implies that if you're happy and content with doing a good job and being paid and rewarded reasonably, then focusing on performance alone is fine. But if 'fine' isn't good enough for you, then working on your image and building your exposure is what's going to make the difference. Step into your boss's boss's shoes for a second and imagine that it's performance review time. The most senior leaders in the business are sat around a table in a drab meeting room. They're doing that awful thing that big businesses do where they go through a list of people in alphabetical order, talk about each person in turn and then decide which performance rating (and therefore what pay rise or bonus) people get paid. If you're fortunate enough to have never come across these meetings before then count yourself lucky - I've lost days of my life to them over the years and it's excruciating. Anyway, you're there as your boss' boss and it's your turn to talk about 'you'. What will you say? What can you say? How much do they actually know about you? The things that are likely to run through their head are:

- Have I met them?
- Do I know what it is they do and how well?
- Have I interacted with them one-on-one?
- Have I heard other people talk about them positively?
- Have they presented to me and/or my peers?

And my personal favourite:

- Have they helped to make me look good? For example, provided information, data, responses to questions, etc.

Behold, the harsh but true reality of getting on in business.

HUSTLING PART ONE: MAKING YOUR BOSS LOOK GOOD

Now stick with me here. I'm not saying you should brown nose or aim to be teacher's pet - what I'm saying is that if you want to play the game, you have to know how the game is played. And that starts with working your way up 'the chain of command' - starting with the person you report to. It's not enough to do your thing and do it well if you want to get on at work. Business is all about relationships - and this starts with the person who signs your pay cheque, the person who vouches for you and represents you to their boss and their boss' boss - your boss.

The easiest and most sure-fire way of having your boss recognise your value and in particular, how invaluable you are, is for them to learn to lean on you. To come to you when they need help and to learn to trust that you will be there to support them. As companies are slimming down, managers and teams are getting more and more work piled on them. Having a trustworthy and capable 'second in command' is a necessity that you can work to your advantage:

- When your boss knows that they can count on you to help them out and make them look good, they're going to trust you more. And when they trust you, they're more likely to give you more responsibilities and opportunities for growth.
- When you're willing to go the extra mile to help your boss out, it demonstrates that you're not just in it for yourself. You're invested in the success of the entire team.
- When your boss looks good, it reflects positively on the team. And when the team is doing well, everyone is happier and more likely to get along. When the senior leaders take notice, they'll begin to look closer at what's behind the good numbers and high team engagement scores - what will they find? You, dear Diva.
- When your boss begins to lean on you, for example, as a sounding board or to help with gathering information for a meeting, they are more likely to mention you to their boss or even their boss's boss. Being mentioned by the right people in the right circles builds your exposure. Suddenly people who didn't know you existed last week are talking about you positively as if they know you!
- When your boss is on holiday or sick - who will *their* boss call on to represent the team at the next leadership meeting?

- Finally, when layoff time comes - if your boss is happy with you and sees you as an asset to the team, then you're less likely to be let go.

But it's not all about saying the right thing, taking the shit and being compliant. If you want your boss to trust you, then you have to show that you have their best interests at heart. Sometimes that means telling them some stuff that they might not want to hear but need to hear. When I think about the best relationships I've had with my bosses in the past, they've been ones that have transcended the typical boss > direct report relationship. They've been ones where I've told them straight about how they're showing up, where they are getting it wrong and how I think they need to play it differently. For example:

- Why did you call a meeting and ask everyone for their ideas when it was clear you'd already made your mind up? It made it look like you were just ticking a box.
- Your need for control is driving people mad, you need to step back and trust that people know what they're doing - otherwise, people are going to get fed up and leave.
- When you said x in that meeting, you made x feel like shit, you might want to go and put that right.
- There's a feeling that you are treating x differently than everybody else and letting

them get away with x. You need to deal with it and make sure everyone knows it.

- People are worried about this recent announcement and they think you know more than you're letting on. I think it would be helpful for you to give an update at the next team meeting.

To be clear, I'm not saying sacrifice any bit of who you are in order to get on or that you should sell your soul to the devil for the benefit of exposure. But there is always a way for you to have your cake and eat it, dear Diva. If you are hungry enough, you'll find it.

Show up as the diva you are - and in doing so, make yourself indispensable.

HUSTLING PART TWO: PLAYING THE CORPORATE GAME

Playing the game at work is about understanding the unwritten rules of the workplace in order to get on. Now, these rules are not found in any employee handbook, but rather in the company culture, politics and relationships between colleagues. If you are going to be successful, then you have to understand the nuances of the workplace and be able to navigate them safely. This is about understanding how decisions are made, who holds the power and how to influence them. It also means knowing when to speak up and when to keep schtum, how to build relationships with colleagues and people more senior than you, and how to present yourself in the best possible light.

It's not about being fake or insincere. It's about understanding that work is not just about doing what's asked of you and meeting deadlines. It's also about building relationships and creating a positive image of yourself. If you do this well, you can gain the respect and trust of people more senior. This can lead to all sorts of opportunities, including promotions, projects, pay rises and most of all - exposure.

While this may involve some level of politicking and calculated manoeuvring, it should never involve compromising on your values - if you ever find yourself in this position, run! To play the game effectively, it's important to step back and notice what you notice. So much insight can be gained from learning about how others have been successful in your company. Something I often say is if you want to become successful quickly, find someone who has achieved the thing that you want and do exactly the same as them - only better.

Observe:
- How do people communicate? What sort of tone do they use? What kind of body language do they adopt? Open and inviting? Or something else?

- How do they approach challenges and deal with a crisis? Do they just get on and make stuff happen? Or do they consult? Who with, how and how often?
- How do they present themselves? What do they wear?
- How do they build relationships? Is it all work and no play? Or do they get to know people? Do they share bits of their personal life as a way of building trust?
- How do they respond to change? Do they wobble? Or do they steady the ship?
- How vulnerable do they allow themselves to be? Do they pretend to know all the answers? Or are they comfortable saying, 'I don't know'?

'The game' will present differently in every company. Only you know how the game is played and won in yours. It starts with being an observer. Tomorrow, at work, sit back and observe - particularly in team meetings. Watch and see who gets the most airtime and to whom the leader in the room pays the most and least attention. Observe who gets a positive response from 'the power' in the room and who might as well have not been there. Treat it all as helpful data.

QUIT MOANING OR DO SOMETHING

Reality check - nobody loves their job 100% of the time. There will always be stuff that you just have to suck up and get on with. Lots of people I meet dream of working for themselves - running a little café, a bookshop, a B&B in the sun. Unless you work long and hard enough to afford yourself the privilege of bringing someone else in to do the hard graft, whilst you swish around doing only the bits you enjoy, you will still have to deal with stuff that you don't like doing. Stuff that doesn't float your boat, that winds you up or that bores the socks off you. Do you think it will all be worth it if you're your own boss? As I write this, I'm thinking about some of my business friends who have managed, through blood, sweat and tears, to elevate themselves to 'swishing stage'. Even that still brings its fair share of headaches: finance, accounts, budgeting, legal obligations, employment issues, liabilities; if your name's above the door, you're on the line - for it all. There's no hiding and burying your head in the sand when the buck stops with you. What I'm saying here is that no matter where you work, what you do or who you work for, there will be stuff that you don't enjoy or that annoys the 'you know what' out of you. Bear this in mind the next time something or someone at work winds you up and you deal with it by paying the job sites a visit - every one of those glossy job ads with their 'competitive salaries' and 'flexible working options' comes with their own downside. And before anyone says that I'm being a pessimist, I'm not. I'm being real. It brings a little bit of sick to my mouth to say what I'm about to say, but it does reinforce my point...

The grass isn't always greener on the other side, dear Diva. It's greener where you water it.

As with most things in life, it comes down to balance.

Balance: An even distribution of weight enabling someone or something to remain upright and steady. If, on balance, the good outweighs the bad, then you're doing OK. If, reflecting objectively, the balance is 80:20 or 70:30 then you're on good ground. Once it starts to tip towards the 60:40, 50:50 and below, then in the words of Whoopi Goldberg, *'You in danger, girl.'*

To get a sense of how well your work is serving you, reflect on the following:

- Why did you take the job to begin with? What did you think it would give you? How was it supposed to benefit you? (Joy, experience, finances, flexibility, exposure?)
- How has it worked out for you? What have you gained? (Or avoided losing.)
- To what degree is it still working for you?

Stepping back and looking at the situation for what it is:

- What's still working in your favour?
- If you were to put your positive knickers on for a second and be extra generous, what positives can you find?
- What isn't working for you?
- What tweaks could be made to make things feel better?

TIPPING POINT

If the balance has tipped or you just aren't feeling the job anymore, before you start looking elsewhere, make sure that you aren't throwing the baby out with the bath water. What I mean is, before you go throwing away whatever good is left to spite the bad, see what can be salvaged. You won't know until you've tried. Ask yourself:

For you to stay, what would need to be different? For example:

- The type of work you do.
- An opportunity or project.
- The team or department you work in.
- Your job title.
- Funding a course of qualification.
- Who you report to.
- A promotion.

- Changes to your working hours.
- Flexible working.
- Salary.

What would it take to keep you?

ASK FOR WHATEVER IT IS YOU NEED

If you knew how common these conversations are you wouldn't think twice about having it. They happen every day of the week in offices all over the world. You don't know about them because why would you? You just see the after-effect; a redistribution of work, this person is moving departments, this person's job title has changed, this person is now studying for this qualification. Just because you don't see them happening, doesn't mean that they aren't happening. I've got to admit that in my own experience, they have (almost) always worked in my favour.

- I'd ask to speak to my line manager, and if they were the problem, I'd ask to speak to their line manager.
- I'd share my thoughts on what was and wasn't working for me. It's all about balance, don't just complain, offer them a shit sandwich.
- I'd offer a solution to the problem, *I've been thinking about x, and if y and/or z were in place then I'm pretty sure I'd feel differently.* Show them that you've done some thinking about this, that you're taking it seriously and that this isn't some whim for the hell of it.

- Lay it out on the table and then check it out with them, *What do you think? Is there something I've missed? Between us, I'm sure that we can come up with something.* Position yourself as a partner in this with them. This isn't something that you're laying at their door for them to solve; it's something that you are willing to work with them on, in order to come to a mutually acceptable agreement.

Sometimes they asked to think about it, but most of the time, if you're speaking to the decision maker, the fear of losing someone who knows what they are doing was enough for them to, let's say, think more 'creatively' about the situation.

It's nice to feel valued and like you are being rewarded fairly for what it is that you bring. The reality is, if pay is your primary issue, then salary hikes aren't always possible, even with the most willing and supportive boss. If the response to your salary request is a no, then have something else in your back pocket ready to go. Investment doesn't always have to equal cash. Investment could mean learning new skills, being coached or mentored by somebody inside or outside the business, funding a development course or qualification, offering flexible working options so that you can spend more time with your family or on your 'side hustles' - more on that later. Flexible working - reducing your hours/days or consolidating your hours, is becoming more and more popular. You might work a longer day four days a week and take the fifth off with no change to salary. It's a brilliant option if you want to start working on your exit strategy.

In my experience, when faced with the prospect of organising my leaving gift:

- Development budgets became available.
- Exciting projects and growth opportunities popped up.
- The option to work more flexibly was on the table.
- 'Back-door' workarounds to rigid 1% pay increase policies suddenly appeared out of nowhere - £ poof £.
- Suddenly it was possible to have the title I wanted and do the work I wanted, when I wanted, on the salary I wanted - without having the responsibility for line managing anybody - I really didn't get on well with line managing people; I have enough to deal with in managing myself, let alone somebody else.

You get the idea. And it kept me going for a year or two until...it didn't. At the point you state clearly and firmly what it is you need in exchange for your precious time, your thinking, your creativity, your presence and your fabulous sense of humour - and the answer is no, then it's time to say, *Thank you and goodbye.*

KNOW YOUR WORTH

When it comes to conversations about money, most of us find it uncomfortable. Either because we aren't used to talking about it - sharing salaries around the dinner table with friends isn't really the done thing, or because we worry that asking for more money will mean we appear greedy or ungrateful for what we have. Then you add on the fear and embarrassment of asking and someone saying no, and it might appear easier to leave and try somewhere new, where they don't know you and if they say no then it doesn't matter, you'll try again somewhere else. Throughout my time in the business world, I was part of many conversations around salary. I observed how the most useless, hopeless, down-downright dumb-assed new hires would join teams on salaries twice what their peers were earning. Two things became clear:

1. Nobody is going to come along and offer you a pay rise out of the goodness of their own heart. If you're sat there on half the salary of your peer doing the same amount of work or more, to the same standard or higher, and you're happily and obediently taking what's offered, staying quiet and not complaining - you're the ideal employee. If only everybody was like you, the exec bonuses would be even bigger! Even the lowest, most unfair and inequitable salaries are no problem at all until the point at which you have something to say about it. At which point...

2. If you ask, you will almost always get. Suddenly it's a case of, *Oh yes, we can see that your salary is lower in comparison; let us do something about that* - as if they're doing you a favour!

Do not feel bad about asking for what it is you need, dear Diva. I'd put my own money on the fact that the person you are asking has had the very same conversation with their boss, and their boss has had the same with theirs. The salary game is one played and won on silence. Bets are hedged on the fact that it's OK to increase salaries in one area because the people in another area aren't asking - so it balances. Don't allow yourself to be on the wrong side of the balance, dear Diva. Speak up and state your worth.

Know your worth. Then add tax.

Tips on asking for what you're worth:

- Unless you know and trust them, don't believe what anybody else tells you about what they earn. You can't rely on people to tell the truth when it comes to matters of money, ego often gets in the way. For this reason, avoid bringing the salaries of other people into the conversation, this is about you, not them.
- Do your homework. Work out what you need to survive and then add on some so you can thrive.

- Research. Look at what similar roles in similar businesses are paying for people with your level of experience and skill.
- Don't be tempted to do yourself down, e.g. *Oh, I don't have this qualification or know how to use that particular system.* Businesses want more and more for less and less. Don't let someone else's fantasy wish list stop you from asserting your right to be rewarded fairly.
- Plan your conversation:
  » Set the scene: I'd like to talk to you about my salary...
  » State the facts: I haven't had a pay rise in x years / I've had a x% pay rise in x years.
  » State the impact: This has made me... struggle to make ends meet / reconsider my place here / look around for better paid work / feel under-appreciated or undervalued.
  » State what you would like instead: For me to...pay my damn bills / feel more valued / feel like I'm being rewarded fairly...this is what I need.
  » Check it out with them: How does that sound?
- Choose a suitable time and place. Face-to-face is always best; you can get a better read from someone than you can online. Of course, if you or your boss are remote, you can make it work

online. Regardless, make sure that you are both somewhere where you won't be distracted. You need a quiet room; the last thing you want is to have this kind of conversation at the side of the desk or on your way to your boss's next meeting (yes, that happened to me).

- Keep the conversation Adult > Adult and assert your needs calmly and respectfully. 'Adult' sounds like, *Here are the facts and this is what I need from you.* 'Child' sounds like, *Please give me more money. I'd be ever so grateful if you did (or throwing a tantrum).* And 'Parent' would sound like, *You've been very naughty by not giving me enough money, so either pay me more or I'll leave (and make you go to your bedroom to think about your actions).* Aim for Adult > Adult.

- Follow up in writing. That way there's a paper trail, and if they start dragging their heels, you'll have something to fall back on.

- Step back and observe how they manage the situation. This is a sign of how much they value you. They have an opportunity here to show themselves in a positive light and demonstrate how they treat people in their business. If they take this stuff seriously, they will keep you updated, you won't have to chase, and they will be fair, honest and transparent - even if the answer is no. If you experience the opposite, then you were right to question your place there to start with and they've just made the decision for you.

Everything you experience, good or bad, is helpful decision making data.

GO FOR THE BLOODY JOB

If you've reached the point where staying has become untenable and you feel that your only option is to leave, then here are my top tips for putting some more diva into your job search:

- Don't jump straight into searching for the kind of job you 'think' you should get - just because you've spent the last 20 years in Sales doesn't mean that you have to spend the next 20 doing the same thing. Stop and think about what it is that you want from your work. See the 'Finding High-Vibe Work Quiz' earlier in this chapter. You could also think about employing the services of a career coach to help you get clearer on the kind of work you want (or don't want) and to help you form an action plan.

- Once you're clear on what it is you want to be doing (or not doing), start trawling through your connections. Think about who you have in your network/entourage that can facilitate email introductions or put in a good word. Don't underestimate the power of your network, dear Diva - besides yourself, it's your greatest asset.

When you find a job you like the look of BLOODY WELL GO FOR IT. Do not, I repeat, DO NOT:

- Be put off by the fantasy wish list of requirements, qualifications or skills. They are almost always pushing their luck and describing someone that doesn't exist. If you tick most of the boxes - apply. What you don't know you can learn. So often I speak to people (mainly women) who find their dream job, tick every box except one and then don't go ahead and apply because they don't meet all the criteria - f*ck the criteria. Anyone in their right mind would snatch you up and pay you good money for the privilege - and you're telling me you're going to let one little requirement stop you from getting the job of your dreams? Please. Allow me to talk in binary terms for a minute. Job hunting is one of the key areas where the difference in mindset between cis-straight male and female is at its most polar. My experience has been that men will look at a job spec, see that they don't meet all (or sometimes any) of the requirements and will apply anyway. Women, on the other hand, diligently go through the lists and if they can't hand on heart say that they meet even one of the requirements, they won't apply. Who ends up getting the job? Mmhm.
- Don't be put off if it says full-time and you want part-time. Unfortunately, even today many

recruiters don't properly consider diversity, equity or inclusion when putting job ads together. More often, they are trying to back-fill a role and replace like-for-like. They're often moving quickly, failing to stop and think about the different ways in which the work could be covered, such as flexible working, job share, hybrid or remote. They just want the same again, but this time with even more experience, qualifications and skills piled on. Don't let their ignorance stand in your way. See it as your responsibility to enlighten them, dear Diva, and show them that they can have what they want, but in a way that works for you too, and that includes flexible working.

- Don't be put off by the salary band. It's all a load of rubbish. As I've said, companies are asking for more and more, for less and less. It's rare to find a company that is willing to pay a decent wage off the bat. Most of the time you have to hustle, I mean...'influence'. If you go in hard and fast and say that you are looking for £10k more than they're advertising, it's likely that the conversation will be brief. Instead, and only if you are genuinely interested in the job, do your research. Look up the salaries of people who already work there. There are websites that allow employees to share their job titles and salaries anonymously and also leave reviews for potential employees to learn what it's really like to work there. Once you've done a bit of 'recruitment recon', enter the process and focus on showing yourself off as best you can. Make them want you, have them picture you working for them, have them fall in love with you, imagining what a difference you will make and all the added value you will bring. Really get them to buy into you, then, when they are complicit in the vision...hit them with your very own list of requirements - salary, pension, perks, company car, annual leave, flexible working, etc. Suss out how far you can push and keep it just on the realistic side of aspirational!

Don't undersell yourself, dear Diva - you can't put a price on magic.

FIND HIGH-VIBE WORK

My darling Diva - you deserve the best, the total best and nothing but the best. You deserve a job that meets you way up where you are. Not a job that you have to make yourself smaller for, to bend and crouch for. You deserve work that:

- Makes you feel more like you.
- Makes you feel happy most of the time.
- Makes the most of your strengths, skills, talents and experience.
- Aligns (or at least doesn't conflict) with the things that are important to you (your values).
- Makes you want to get up each day and say, *Come on world, let's be havin' you.*

Most of all, you deserve work that *works* for you.

To help you find 'high-vibe work', consider these questions:

- What have you always dreamt of doing for work but never dared to admit to anybody?
- What have been the happiest and most fulfilling moments in your career so far? What were you doing? Or not doing? Consider creating a version of the Happiness Timeline for your career. See the chapter titled 'Happiness'. Once complete, step back and ask yourself, how can I bring more of these things into my next career move?
- Using the Goals That Make You Go Oooh model from the chapter titled 'Goals', think about these questions:
  - » What brings me joy?
  - » What brings me a sense of meaning/purpose?
  - » What makes the most of my strengths?

- What do you care most about? How could you find a way for these things to play a part in how you earn a living?
- Now bear with me. This question is often overused but is effective...If you knew that you couldn't fail, how would you make a living?
- What would it take for you to stop making a living and instead, make a life? Ooh.
- If you had 100% total free will, how would you choose to make a living? Really think about this one. There are very few superpowers that come with this existence, dear Diva - but the ability to choose our own path, to make our own decisions and go and do what we damn well please, that's one. Remember it's there; keep it in your back pocket and don't be afraid to use it.

FLIP IT 'TIL IT WORKS FOR YOU

So, your job isn't doing it for you. You've got an exit plan, whether it's weeks, months, or years down the line, and all you need to do is bide your time until your next move. Rather than being miserable about how things are, start applying your diva mindset to your current situation. I don't mean go around making crazy demands and wearing your sunglasses to meetings (although I could get on board with the sunglasses). I mean, start applying a success mindset to what you've got going for you right now. I'll let you into a conversation I had with a dear friend of mine recently. He's taken a job, only to discover that it's not what he thought it was or was sold, and he's finding himself doing what he considers entry-level work. Now he's being paid well, which was part of the appeal, but the work he's doing is what he was doing ten years ago and definitely not worthy of his salary. We get talking and it's not long before he's sharing his dissatisfaction and that he feels trapped. If he leaves now, then he's worried it won't look good on his CV and he's already agreed with his husband that he's in it for at least 12-18 months. So, we're talking and the conversation goes like this:

Me: So, what are the positives?

Him: There aren't any, it's shit.

Me: There has to be something. Come on, try and find one positive.

Him: Well, apart from the money, I have met some high-profile people, people I never thought I'd meet. We've even exchanged numbers.

Me: OK, what else?

Him: They've paid for me to do a publishing course...

Me: Great, and is that something you could use after you leave?

Him: Yes. Thinking about it, I've also learned a lot about editing. I've always felt like a bit of an imposter before, but now I feel like I'm actually understanding it.

Me: Well, that doesn't sound bad to me - more connections, more qualifications, more skills, more confidence *and* more money? What's the problem?

Him: The problem is I'm back to doing copywriting, and the job title's rubbish. I feel like I've gone back ten years.

Me: OK, who else does what you do? And are you 'just' doing copywriting or is there more to it?

Him: No, it's just me. I've been told it's my publication... and I suppose there is more to it. I do everything, not just the writing.

Me: So, you don't 'just' do copywriting. What would a more accurate and befitting job title be? Editor?

Him: Ooh, I like that, yes - Editor (I could see the cogs turning at this point).

Me: OK, so if you were to big it up whilst still keeping it real, but perhaps embellishing ever so slightly around the edges, what's the story you are going to start telling yourself?

Him: (After a few minutes and with a little bit of

prompting from me) I'm the Editor of this up and coming publication. They pay me well for what I do. I get to meet all these well-known people. The company invests in me and my development. It's a great thing to have on my CV and once I decide that my time is up, I can use all this experience and my new connections wherever I go next. Hmm, maybe it's not so bad after all.

Me: You don't say...

And that, dear Diva, is how you flip it 'til it works for you. I'm not saying lie or delude yourself, but find and accentuate what good there is. Good that can be of use to you wherever you go next. Wherever you work and whatever you do, you have a choice. You can take what's given to you (title, work, etc) and represent it as it's been represented to you, or you can flip it 'til it works a bit better for you.

Maybe you've come across LinkedIn, the social networking site for businesspeople? Looking at people's profiles in the search results, it's clear who is simply representing their work as it's been handed to them, and who is flipping it. Don't get me wrong, you can go too far and it becomes blatantly obvious when people do. But if you are going to represent your career online, be sure to stay on the ambitious end of accurate.

Hetal:

Real Life: Primary School Teacher.

LinkedIn: Early Years Expert with Over 20 Years of Teaching Experience.

Ruth:

Real Life: Purchasing Assistant.

LinkedIn: Procurement Professional with Knowledge of X, Y, Z.

Sally:

Real Life: Freelance Graphic Designer.

LinkedIn: Founder and CEO of Doodles by Sally. Award-Winning Businesswomen and Entrepreneur.

Raminder:

Real Life: Sales Manager.

LinkedIn: Regional Sales Manager with a Passion for Developing People and Teams.

Don't lie, just do yourself justice. If it makes your time at work just a little more tolerable - then it's worth it.

Have the balls to back yourself.

START A SIDE HUSTLE

Unless you're financially secure enough to be able to quit your unfulfilling job and start anew, the best route I've found to creating a more fulfilling career for yourself is through a side hustle. What on earth is a side hustle, you ask? It's something that you get paid to do alongside your main job. Of course, the first thing you need to find is time. Whether it's evenings, weekends or a non-working day in the week, that's all you really need to get started.

Use your weekend to build the life you want, instead of trying to escape the life you have.

Picture this. You're employed full-time as a software developer, but you dream of creating and launching your own tech business:

- You can be upfront with your employer about your aspirations and let them know that you're going to be spending your non-working time developing your business...or you say it's none of their damn business and tell them when you need to.
- Ideally you want to make sure that contractually you are allowed to earn money elsewhere. Check your contract, some cover it, some don't - although as people are finding more and more creative ways to earn a living, businesses

are getting savvy about protecting their own assets, intellectual property and clients - they might not like the idea of you using your time and expertise elsewhere, especially if you are using equipment they've provided or if there's potential for you to take clients away from them in the future.

- Start small. Don't spend money on things that you don't need to. You don't need a fancy website or an expensive logo. Start by developing your proof of concept - will people actually pay you to do this stuff yourself?

- Be willing to do some free work in return for testimonials or case studies from reputable names that you can show on your (future) website.

- Develop your side hustle to the point where the balance becomes tipped in your favour. This is the point where you have so much of your own work that something has to give. At this point, you could look at reducing your hours so that you're able to give more time to your ever-expanding side hustle (which is what I did). This might be the time to come clean if you haven't been transparent to this point or you quit your day job, having developed something that you know can work and most importantly, can pay your bills.

—CHAPTER TEN—

BEWARE THE BITCHES

*A diva knows that it's the best fruit
the birds pick at.*

BEWARE THE BITCHES

Bitches are the polar opposite of Divas. Whereas the Diva stands for love, kindness and compassion, Bitches perpetuate hate and jealousy. They are lazy. Rather than doing the work to understand themselves and their place in the world, they prefer to spend their time attempting to bring others down. They will attempt to bring you down, dear Diva – to point out your perceived flaws and to dim your light in an attempt to make themselves feel better. Deal with it as a diva – safe in the knowledge that their behaviour has absolutely nothing to do with you, and absolutely everything to do with them.

You could try to help them see the error of their ways; you may even suggest that they read this book. Maybe they'll listen, maybe they won't. The only thing you can control is your response to their negativity. Appreciating that this approach is sometimes easier said than done, the pages that follow include some of my favourite and most frequently reached for quotes and quips relating to these unenlightened souls. When it comes to dealing with the Bitches, the less said, the better. I'll let the quotes do the talking.

BEWARE THE BITCHES

Don't take criticism from anybody you
wouldn't take advice from.

When you think people are talking about you,
just remember - all publicity is good publicity.

The only way to avoid criticism is to do nothing,
say nothing and be nothing - Aristotle

It's better to be hated for who you are, than to be
loved for someone you're not. It's a sign of your
worth sometimes if you're hated by the right
people - Bette Davis

Pay no attention to people talking behind
your back. For to criticise is the easiest thing
in the world. It requires very little thought,
imagination or intellect.

Whoever is trying to bring you down
is already beneath you.

If someone goes out of their way to do you
wrong. Know this. They'll be dead one day.

If everyone likes you, you're pretty dull
- Bette Davis

When presented with unsolicited feedback,
accept it graciously, then wipe your arse with
it.

Don't be distracted by criticism. Remember - the
only taste of success some people get is to take
a bite out of you - Zig Ziglar

Thinking is difficult, that's why
most people judge - Carl Young

When people show you who
they really are, believe them.

When they go low, we go high - Michele Obama

If you knew how often people deal with their
shit by projecting it onto others, you would
learn to take almost nothing personally.

CHAPTER ELEVEN

HAPPINESS

A diva knows that happiness is something to be created, not to be found.

HAPPINESS

...happiness cannot be pursued; it must ensue, and it only does so as the unintended side-effect of one's personal dedication to a cause greater than oneself - Viktor Frankl

As a diva, you bring joy to the lives of others by living unapologetically as yourself, by loving yourself. Through this, you show others that it is possible for them to love themselves too. You shine your light into places where there may have been little light before. You offer yourself as the touch paper to the dimming flame of another.

Who doesn't want to be happy? Who in their right mind would seek out people and situations that bring them unhappiness? Nobody. And yet so often, people find themselves 'tolerating'. Tolerating things, situations and people that bring them the total opposite of happiness. Tolerance is a tricky bitch. It starts out well-meaning, for example, *I'll put up with this situation because it's the easier/kinder thing to do. I don't want to make a fuss.* But it isn't long before our capacity to tolerate expands and we begin to tolerate more than we care to. It seeps its way into other areas of our life and the well-intentioned benefits of tolerating become outweighed by the sheer weight and discomfort it brings.

When you live a busy life, as most of us do, it can be all too easy to take your eye off your happiness dial. The things in your life which bring you joy, no matter how big or small, get replaced with the Three Bitches of the Apocalypse:

- Should.
- Must.
- Need.

I've got a free half-hour; I really 'should' do that. I 'must' do that. I 'need' to do that. Even the smallest joys are replaced by obligations or things that benefit everybody except yourself.

It might be that you're tolerating situations or people due to fear. Fear of what change might bring - the unknown. Will I be able to make it? Do I have what it takes to go it alone? Will I survive? If this sounds like you, then listen up. You will do more than survive, dear Diva - you will thrive. But first, you must let go of whatever or whoever is holding you back. See the chapters titled, 'Standing Up For Yourself', 'Failure' and 'Self-Sabotage'.

Like confidence, happiness is not a 'thing' which can be sought. In fact, the pursuit of happiness is said to only lead one way, as fellow diva LuLu once said:

The pursuit of happiness is the source of all unhappiness.

Your happiness is a direct consequence of the choices you make. This means:

- The people you choose to surround yourself with - and yes, that includes family.
- The partner you choose.
- How you choose to earn a living.
- How you choose to spend your downtime.
- Where you choose to live.
- What you choose to wear.
- How you choose to talk to yourself.
- The degree to which you choose to be of service to others.

As well as not being a thing in and of itself, neither is happiness experienced the same way by any two people. The things that bring me happiness will be different to the things that bring you happiness. The cocktail will look and taste different for each of us.

Ask yourself:

- What and who brings me happiness?
- Which of my choices contribute positively towards my happiness?
- Which don't? What's the price I pay?
- What choices could I make to bring myself a bit more happiness?
- If my best friend was answering these questions on my behalf, what would they say? Ask them.

Remember, dear Diva, that you are always at choice. It might not always be obvious, but if you look beneath the surface, you will see that you are and have always been, the master of your own destiny. You are in the driving seat - you choose the direction and you also choose who you bring along for the ride.

- You don't like a situation? Change it.
- Your job isn't bringing you joy? Change it.
- Don't like how you talk to yourself sometimes? Change it.
- You aren't happy with your partner? Change them.

OK, that last one was a joke (maybe).

Life is too darn short to tolerate anything or anyone that doesn't put a big fat smile on your face each day.

WHAT'S YOUR DEFINITION OF HAPPINESS?

A simple question, perhaps. Perhaps not. If you haven't given much thought to this in a while, then maybe it's time that you did. The thing is, you are always changing and evolving. Think about the person you were just a decade ago:

- What were you like?
- What did you enjoy doing?
- What did you do for work?
- What hobbies or interests did you have?
- What was important to you?
- How does that compare to who you are today?
- If you could talk to your past self right now, what would you say to them?

People change. You will have changed. Perhaps not drastically, but enough to make a difference. Thinking about the person you are now:

- What is your definition of happiness?
- When you're in your 'happy place', what are you doing? Who are you with? (Or not with.)
- What are you not doing?
- If that image of happiness is a ten on a scale, where's your current level of happiness?
- What needs to change?

Remember. One small step forward is worth more than a thousand good intentions.

STATE OF MIND?

I think there is something to be said about happiness being a state of mind. It can be easy to lose sight of the things that we have going for us, particularly when times get tough. The bad can sometimes cast a shadow on the good and if positivity isn't your natural strength, then one can find oneself in a pit of despair when actually things aren't that bad - see the chapter titled 'Worrying' if any of this resonates with you. Of course, it's not as simple as thinking positive thoughts and all will be well again. But trying to look for the joy in a situation, the positive, the upside - will no doubt help. Like most things, practise makes perfect. If this isn't your natural go-to approach, then it might not come easy, but give it a go. In any given situation, you have a choice. You can wallow in the shittiness of it, or you can accept it for what it is, recognise what you can and can't control, find the light and move towards it.

I choose my mood and I choose to be happy.
- Julie Pates

Julie is an old work colleague of mine whose words I've carried with me for not far off 20 years. Thank you, Julie.

THE GUEST HOUSE BY RUMI

These words by 13th century poet, Rumi, perfectly sum up the opportunity that we have, even in the tough times, to welcome something new into our lives. How you choose to see things, dear Diva, can make all the difference.

This being human is a guest house.

Every morning a new arrival.

A joy, a depression, a meanness, some momentary awareness comes as an unexpected visitor.

Welcome and entertain them all!

Even if they are a crowd of sorrows, who violently sweep your house empty of its furniture,

still, treat each guest honourably.

They may be clearing you out for some new delight.

The dark thought, the shame, the malice,

meet them at the door laughing,

and invite them in.

Be grateful for whoever comes,

because each has been sent as a guide from beyond.

WHAT HAVE YOU GOT GOING FOR YOU?

How easy do you find it to talk positively about yourself and your achievements? If you answered *very easy,* then I'd have more reason for concern than if you'd answered *somewhat* or *not at all.* If it feels a little uncomfortable, if it doesn't come totally naturally to you, if you don't love to talk about yourself, then congratulations - the chances are you're probably not a dick. The flip side to that positive is that you run the risk of downplaying your successes. The word of the day here is 'balance'. You should be able to recognise your hard work, the things you've achieved, the hardships you've endured. And you should be able to draw happiness from all the times that you tried and succeeded. These are things to remind yourself of when you're feeling down in the dumps, when things are tough or when you just need to turn that frown upside down.

Not that you require it, but you have full permission to big yourself up here. I want you to throw yourself into this next bit and enjoy it. Grab yourself some paper and write down all the things that you've got going for you in your life. No matter how small, they all add up. Go with whatever comes to mind. You can include anything you like. Here are some examples to get you started:

- Skills / Talents.
- Qualifications / Awards.
- Goals achieved.
- Career achievements.
- People in your life.
- Difficulties overcome.
- Things that bring you joy.
- Times you've been brave.

Keep this in your back pocket.

Credit: Barefoot Coaching

Abundance is realising that others would kill for what you already have.

SMALL JOYS

Often, it's the small things that make the biggest difference and that's also true when it comes to happiness. Little things like a long soak in a hot bath, speaking to a friend on the phone, cosy weekends spent with a good book, muddy walks with the dog, or the sound of rain on a caravan roof, can bring so much joy. If you're in tune with yourself, then you may find that you instinctively reach for these little things when you need to put a smile back on your face. If you've lost touch with the small joys in your life, then it's worth reminding yourself of them and then making time for them.

Make time for the small things. Because one day you will realise that the small things were in fact the big things.

HAPPINESS TIMELINE - LOOK BACK, TO MOVE FORWARD

You know the drill by now. Draw a line that represents a period of time that makes sense to you. It could be the last week, month, year or decade!

Think about periods within that timeline where you felt at your happiest and plot them.

For each point, reflect on the following:

- What were you doing?
- Who were you with?
- Specifically, what was it about the situation that made you feel happy?
- You might also like to reflect on the degree to which your personal values were being fulfilled at that time. See the chapter titled 'Standing Up For Yourself' to discover, or rediscover, more about the things that are important to you.

Once complete, step back and observe any patterns or themes which stand out to you.

What actions could you take to bring more of that happiness into your life right now? That might include the things you were doing, things you were not doing, or the types of people you were with.

GRATITUDE

Now if you're rolling your eyes at the idea of being grateful for the things that you have in your life, hear me out. Yes, gratitude has been over-popularised in recent years and has gotten swept up in what's become known as the 'toxic positivity' movement on social media, but it does have its place. It's said that your brain can't process anxiety and gratitude at the same time. So, even if the practice of giving thanks for the good stuff doesn't change the bad stuff, if it distracts the mind for a little, well then surely that's a good thing, right? And if some of the warm and fuzzies then happen to make their way in, even better. It's also said to be catching. The more you recognise, the more you will find. Give it a go.

GRATITUDE QUESTIONS

- What and who are you grateful for in your life right now?
- What might you be taking for granted?
- What small joys are you grateful for?
- What or who made you smile recently?
- What simple pleasure did you enjoy today?

The universe likes gratitude. A bit like a friend who gives you a gift that you don't like, if you say 'I hate it, it's awful' - that friend isn't going to give you another gift. If you say, 'I love it, thank you so much', that friend is much more likely to give you another gift when they see something they think you will like.
- Louise Hay

SPREAD THE JOY: WRITE SOME FAN MAIL

If you've ever received kind words from somebody in a letter, email or text out of the blue, then you will know how good it feels. If sharing the love makes you happy too, then it's a win-win. Consider spreading the joy and writing some fan mail of your very own.

Think of somebody who has done something to help you recently, or perhaps not so recently! Take a moment to write them a message and let them know how their words or actions have impacted positively on you. Maybe make it a regular thing. The world needs more happiness and kindness in it. You, dear Diva, may just be offering somebody a gift at the exact time they require it the most.

GIVE FEWER F*CKS

If you find that worrying or ruminating on unhelpful thoughts or worst-case scenarios is getting in the way of you living your best life, then I offer you this:

*Give fewer f*cks. So much unhappiness and sadness in life can be avoided by simply giving fewer f*cks. If you've spent your whole life giving unnecessary f*cks, then it might feel difficult to suddenly stop. Start today by giving one less f*ck. Then tomorrow, give two less f*cks. The third day, three less f*cks. It won't be long before you find yourself giving far fewer f*cks than before.*

The secret to being happy is letting every situation be what it is, rather than what you think it should be.

— CHAPTER TWELVE —

KINDNESS

*A diva understands that kindness
is really all there ever is.*

KARMA

Let's begin with a little science.

For every action in nature, there has to be an equal and opposite reaction.

Newton's Third Law: Action & Reaction

Isaac Newton, huh? What a diva.

Here's the thing. Karma's a bitch. But she's no ordinary bitch. She can run 10,000 metres faster than Mo Farah and do it in 10-inch heels. She will come for you quicker than any other bitch on the planet and what's more? She never forgets. If you put shit out to the world, if you're shitty to others - she knows where you live. And she will deliver your shit back to you ten-fold.

Ye reap what ye sow, ho.

When it comes to kindness, that's really all there is to know - don't be a dick. And if you take only one thing from this book, let it be this - do no harm. If you aspire to more, and hopefully you do, then make it your business to do good in the world.

Intent is everything. It's the difference between a well-meaning mistake and a conscious act of cruelty. When it comes to kindness, the same is true. If the intent behind your kindness is to receive, if it's driven by a selfish or self-fulfilling need or desire, then karma will see straight through it. She is pure, unadulterated universal energy, baby. She's been around since before time was time, and what's more, she's the biggest diva of all. If you think you can piss in her tea and tell her it's raining, you've got another thing coming. Give with no expectation of return, not because of who the other person is or what they can do for you, but because of who you are.

SHOWING KINDNESS TO YOURSELF

From airlines telling you to put your own oxygen mask on first before helping others, to the likes of the superstar drag queen RuPaul saying, *'If you can't love yourself, how the hell you gonna love someone else?'* and countless Instagram self-help 'experts' reminding you that you can't pour from an empty cup, we're told to start by taking care of ourselves before attempting to help others. But we don't. Well, that's not entirely true. If you want to experience good examples of self-kindness, just look to the LGBTQ+ community. We've got it down pretty well, and you know what? We're all the better off for it. Not because we are selfish, but because we've learnt the hard way. In a shitty world where bitches are coming for you - and in our case add to that institutions, governments, religion, legislation and so on. In a world where it's still illegal to be LGBTQ+ in 64 countries and in 12 of those you can be given the death penalty for loving who you love, in a world where it's barely 50 years since homosexuality was declassified a 'disease', we've learnt that the fiercest weapon against cruelty, is kindness. In order to get by, to survive, we've had to get up each morning, look ourselves in the mirror and say, *You've got this - pretty bitch.*

Kindness to oneself is a choice. When you get home after a long day at work, you walk in the door, dump your bag and kick off your shoes; you have a choice. You can pick up the hoover and begin working through your list of chores: cleaning, tidying, cooking dinner, taxiing the kids around. Or you can make yourself a drink, sit down and take 10 minutes to yourself. You can say to your other half, *It's your turn tonight,* then go upstairs, run yourself a hot bath, turn the music up loud and lock the bathroom door.

So, in what ways can you show a bit more kindness to yourself?

- What routines do you look forward to? How can you increase the frequency and depth of these?
- When you're having 'me time', what are your favourite things to do?
- What activities make you feel more like yourself? When did you last do any of them?
- Who does it feel good to be around? Who could you indulge in a bit of self-kindness with? (I didn't mean that how it sounded.)

Make a list and then make a plan. Stick to your guns and if anyone should try and steer you away from that plan, from your 'self-kindness time', let them experience the force of a diva.

The other thing to note here is that no flower blooms all year round. What you need from yourself in January will be different to what you need in June and different again in October. Think about how your self-kindness looks throughout the year and what becomes more or less important as the seasons change.

Don't forget that when you need a boost and for whatever reason, you aren't able to get there for yourself, take a look at your Bad Bitch Board or read some of your fan mail. Failing that, reach for your entourage rolodex and give your 'Hype Person' a call - they'll know just the thing you need to hear.

KINDNESS TO OTHERS

The world needs kindness. Furthermore, the world needs your kindness. No act of kindness, no matter how small, is ever wasted. We never know what the person next to us is really going through. Sometimes one small act of kindness is all it takes to change a person's life. And being kind is actually cool. Not only that, but it spreads. If you see someone without a smile, lend them one of yours. Then watch as they do the same for the next person. Before you know it, your small act of kindness has created a ripple effect which extends far beyond yourself. Nobody knows where or from whom it originated and nobody cares. They simply receive it and pass it on - that's the point.

Remember that some of the people you encounter this week with the biggest smiles and the funniest jokes are going through the darkest, loneliest and most painful battles - the safest bet is to be kind to everyone - Steven Bartlett

There is no such thing as an ordinary life. By creation, you and the people around you, are each extraordinary. One of a kind. You've each been through stuff, and you are each going through stuff. Sorrow, grief, misery and disease do not discriminate. We each live, experience and then die. Nobody is above or below another - we are equal. And equally deserving of the very best things in life. Some of us are more privileged than others. Maybe that's down to the luck of the draw (to whom we were born) or maybe that's down to the choices we made. Regardless, nobody in 2023, or any other year for that matter, deserves to experience sadness, despair, depression, loneliness, loss, homelessness or any of the other shitty things that can, and undoubtedly will, come our way at some point. We will only ever see the tip of the iceberg, the bits that people are comfortable putting out to the world, the mask that conceals the swirling tides below. We, *you*, have the opportunity to make a positive difference to the lives of others. You already will be doing for those you love, but I'm not talking about them. I'm talking about complete strangers. People whom you have never met and will likely never meet again. The next time you are out for coffee, stop and look around. Notice the people sitting around you. How do they seem? What do you think is going through their mind? Do they seem happy? Sad? Are they worried about something? If they're upset, then that might be a give-away, but the truth is, you never know. Make it your business then to show kindness to each and every person you meet. Leave a gorgeous trail of shimmering gold dust wherever you go and as it touches complete strangers, let it leave them with a smile.

Don't look down on anybody unless you're going to pick them up - Andrew, Adam's Dad

WHAT DO YOU NEED FROM ME RIGHT NOW?

You know, one of the nicest things you can do for a person is to be what they need you to be in their moment of need. Have you ever gone running to a friend for a good old rant and then been left feeling well and truly peeved when all they did was try to fix the situation? By fix, I mean they offered you advice or tried to calm you down by encouraging you to think rationally. Whilst they may well have been trying to help, if all you wanted at that moment was to get things off your chest, unload and then crack on with your day, then you were probably left feeling:

a. Annoyed that they didn't just sit and listen.
b. Pretty miffed that you were robbed of the opportunity to have a good old moan!

Sometimes there's no better stress relief than having a bitch with your bestie, saying what needs to be said, getting it off your chest and then skipping merrily into the rest of your day feeling a whole lot lighter.

The next time somebody comes to you with a problem and you feel the urge to offer advice - STOP. Before you jump in, ask the person:

• Do you want to be helped? (Offer advice/help them to see things from another angle).
• Do you want to be hugged? (This speaks for itself).
• Do you want to be heard? (Shut up and listen).

The first time you ask somebody this question, they might be a bit confused about what it is you are asking them. They might not know how to respond. In that case, 'shut up and listen' is your safest bet. Practise making it clear what you need from those around you before diving into conversation, so that they get used to the idea. You might find that the next time they come to you with something, they tell you what they need from you right at the start, e.g. *OK, I need to have a rant; I just want you to listen.*

Caution: Rant in Progress!

RESIST THE FIX

If having read the section above, you are wondering whether you might be a fixer, this next bit is for you.

As uncomfortable as this may be to hear, nobody in your life - past, present or future, needed/needs you to fix them. This includes your partner, your friends, your colleagues, your kids, your taxi driver and the stranger sitting next to you on the train. Even your most messed-up friends and family members do not need you to fix them. Just allow them to be. You do you and let them do them.

You may be thinking, *But I love them, I want them to be happy* - stop. If people want your help, trust that they will ask for it. The truth is, many people who complain about being unhappy are, in fact, happy being unhappy. For whatever reason, being unhappy is working for them on some level. Trying to change them therefore is a futile endeavour. All that will happen is you will exhaust yourself attempting to fix someone who doesn't want (or isn't ready) to be fixed. Remember the saying, 'You can lead a horse to water but you can't make it drink'? Well, the same applies here. The best thing, for both of you, is to accept them as you find them. Don't try to make things better for them. Don't try to mend, repair, patch up or fix them. Just be there for them. Offer them a shoulder to cry on and show kindness, empathy, compassion and humility; until such a time as you've had enough of being there for them. At the point you find yourself complaining to others about somebody else's complaining, it's you who has a choice to make, dear Diva.

You can put up and shut up, or in the interest of your own boundaries and wellbeing - you can tap out and back out.

Don't waste your time attempting to fix people. Instead, turn your attention inward and fix whatever is inside you that is making you want to fix others.

COMPASSION

Compassion is said to be the currency of kindness. When times are tough, having somebody show up with something as simple as a text that says, *I'm thinking of you*, can make all the difference. Offering a generous ear to somebody and having them speak without question or judgment, can help lighten the load that we didn't even know we were carrying.

Humans are social animals. We aren't designed to exist alone. Showing compassion towards somebody sends them a clear message that they are seen, they are loved and they aren't alone.

Compassion, of course, can come easier to some than others. For example, whilst I'm highly empathetic and I find it easy to relate to what somebody might be experiencing, I have to work at being compassionate. With practise, I've found it easier to be sensitive towards others and to offer them the space and the words they need to work through what they are experiencing. I had to unlearn what compassion meant to me. I'd avoided it for so long because I falsely believed that it was all about entertaining misery and talking in depth about feelings and emotions, e.g. *Oh gosh, yes, isn't it all so awful. No wonder you feel like you do. I'd just give up now if I was you.* If you ask Google to define compassion, this is what you get back - 'Sympathetic pity and concern for the sufferings or misfortunes of others.' Grim huh? Why would you want to entertain that? What I've realised is that it isn't about misery and pity at all. It's about showing up for somebody in their hour of need. It's about remembering that we each experience the world differently and that we never truly know the full picture - there's always more going on than meets the eye. So, when you come across someone who is struggling and you are faced with the choice of whether to lean in or to walk away - lean in. Ask them how they are and when they respond, ask again. This time, *How are you really?* And offer them a safe space to share what's going on for them. You don't have to entertain the misery and you don't have to seek a solution. Just let them know that you are there.

- How easy do you find it to show compassion?
- In which situations or with whom do you find it easier?
- Think of somebody you know who is going through something. In what ways could you show even a small amount more compassion towards them?

Be a lamp, a lifeboat, a ladder. Help someone's soul heal. Walk out of your house like a shepherd - Rumi

KINDNESS TO ANIMALS

Animals are without ego. They love unconditionally. They are selfless creatures. They don't hold grudges, they don't set out to destroy and they certainly don't start wars. Their senses are highly tuned and they are in touch with their environment and the other living creatures around them. They know when we are sad, when we are happy, when we are grieving and when we are stressed. However they find us, they meet us where we are and they offer us their unwavering love. Their motivation is to take what they need to survive and nothing more. Even after severe ill-treatment at the hands of humans, they will seek comfort from the same hand that hurt them. Far from being inferior, animals are enlightened beings, free from the constraints of what it means to have a human existence on this planet. Their behaviour is something to aspire toward.

Ultimately, showing compassion towards animals will help you become more compassionate towards people. Treat animals with empathy, care, respect and dignity - or leave them alone. The same, of course, is true for how you treat humans.

Stand up for those who have no voice. Show them kindness, hold them close and show them that they are loved as much as they love. To you, they are part of your world. But to them, you are their whole world.

You can tell a lot about a person by how they treat animals.

I've never met an animal I didn't like, and I can't say the same thing about people.
- Doris Day

RANDOM ACTS

I've made it my business to carry out random acts of kindness each day. Small things like complimenting something that someone is wearing, *That colour looks really good on you.* Or showing an interest in someone working behind a till in a store, *How's your day been so far?* When you take the time to focus your attention on another, something happens - people feel seen. They are reminded that they are important too and that they matter.

It's cool to be kind. Listen to people, show an interest. Ask them a question about themselves. Pay them a compliment and watch them light up.

Random acts of kindness come in all shapes and sizes. Here are just a few, but know that it's not really about what you do; it's about just doing something.

Zero Cost:

- Give an unexpected compliment.
- Take an interest in somebody, particularly those working in service roles: stores, hotels, restaurants, etc.
- Let somebody go ahead of you in a queue.
- Let somebody out of a traffic junction.
- Give up your seat to somebody on public transport.

- Ask somebody about themselves, particularly the elderly. Help them to remember the good old days.
- Check in on your neighbour.
- Donate unwanted clothes, toys or items to your local donation bank / charity shop.
- Volunteer at a charity shop / school / homeless shelter etc.
- Open the door for someone.
- Write a lovely small business review online.
- Mow your neighbour's lawn.
- Offer to mentor somebody.

Small / Medium Cost:

- Leave a small tip in a restaurant or café - always hand it directly to your server, look them in the eye and thank them.
- Pay for someone else's coffee.
- Bake someone a cake.
- Buy flowers for your local nursing home.
- Buy a little bit of something for your postman/woman/person.
- Leave some change in a vending machine.
- Donate food to your local food bank.
- Donate to your local homeless shelter or animal rescue, etc.
- Keep a spare umbrella to give to somebody in the rain.
- Leave a basket of balls at your local dog park.

Carry out a random act of kindness with no expectation of reward, safe in the knowledge that one day, someone might do the same for you.
- Princess Diana

SEND SOME FAN MAIL

It's easy to assume that people know how grateful we are to them. But that's not always the case. Think of somebody whose words or actions have had a profound impact on you, life-changing perhaps. How much of an idea do you think they have about the impact they've had on you? Perhaps to them, they were just going about their business, doing what they do, showing up positively and paying kindness forward - role modelling what it means to be a diva. Do they have any idea just how much they've helped you? And what that help has led you to achieve? Probably not. If you are in any doubt, then I encourage you to let them know before it's too late. Your random act of kindness might just be the boost that they weren't expecting, but that they desperately need.

IF YOU CAN, GIVE. IF YOU CAN'T, RAISE

When it comes to charity, money really does make the world go round. Many charities don't get a look in when it comes to government grants or funding; they don't have the resources required to even apply for it. If you can, give. I'm not talking much; a single pound coin can make a difference to the charities out there struggling to provide services. Services that at any point any one of us could find ourselves relying on. If you aren't able to give, then raise. Do a sponsored walk or put on a cake sale at work.

Your support will matter deeply to charities around the UK that are struggling to stay afloat.

Alone we can do so little; together we can do so much – Helen Keller

—CHAPTER THIRTEEN—

KEEPING YOUR COOL

A diva knows that the problem is almost never the problem, and almost always the way they are thinking about the problem.

KEEPING YOUR COOL

Even as the most self-aware diva armed with the knowledge and awareness of what triggers the 'you know what' out of you (See Knowing Yourself) - people will still get your goat. Most of the time their intentions will be well-meaning. People don't always think before they speak and at times will act without thinking about the knock-on effect. Or, on occasion, someone may be out to get you. Try as you may, you are only human. At times, you will react in the moment or hold back, wishing that you hadn't. These situations are all part of the human experience designed to deepen your awareness of yourself and, if managed well, to deepen connections with others. They are opportunities to learn and to grow, even though they might not feel like that at the time. Whatever it is that's pissed you off: your car arrives late, someone's sent you an arsey email and has copied in the boss, Janet just commented on how you've left 'early' the last few days without knowing you'd worked all weekend - whatever it is, you are always at choice and therefore you are the one in control. Here are six things that I've found helpful to remind myself of over the years. Keep them in your back pocket and in the heat of the moment, bring them to your attention:

1. Behind every action is a positive intent - it may not always be obvious.
2. Hurt people hurt people.

3. Nobody can make you feel a certain way. That's something you control.
4. Emotions are merely suggestions as to how you could react; you always have a choice.
5. Usually the simplest explanation is the correct one (Occam's Razor). Usually that amounts to people just not thinking before they open their mouths.
6. There's always more going on than meets the eye. It's unlikely that this situation is actually about you.

The car was late because the driver is having chemotherapy and felt ill that morning. The boss got copied into that email because the sender had just had a poor performance review and was told that they need to be more transparent with what they are working on. Aside from being a cow, Janet's just been pulled up for leaving early herself, except the boss knows that she's not making up the time.

People are very rarely outright nasty. Assume positive intent - then have them prove you right.

STRESS RESPONSES

When that fabulous brain of yours perceives danger, it automatically and immediately prepares your body for one of four stress responses:

Fight / Flight: These are active defence responses. Your heart rate gets faster, increasing oxygen flow to your muscles. Your pain reception decreases and your senses, particularly your hearing, heighten. You are ready to either take a bitch down or run for the hills, baby.

Freeze / Fawn: These are passive defence responses. The psychological response is similar but this time you lock up and freeze. If you stay still long enough, the threat might just carry on straight past you. Or perhaps the path of least resistance is to fawn - to succumb to give in and get this over with as quickly as possible.

These aren't conscious decisions that you make, they happen in the blink of an eye and your brain is running on autopilot in an attempt to keep you alive. Of course, in a modern-day setting, an office, for example, your options are limited. If an arsey email comes in that really gets your back up, you aren't going to actually get into a scrap with the sender. You aren't going to get up from your desk and run out of the building, although that would be pretty epic if you did. Instead, the 'fight' might come from replying to the email in the heat of the moment with an equally arsey response, or perhaps the 'flight' response might be to close down your emails and take a look at the BBC News website instead. 'Freeze' might be just staring at the screen unable to bring yourself to respond. Meanwhile, 'fawn' might be replying with a very pleasant response, giving in to all demands and probably starting with, *Sorry*... The email isn't a threat. It might dent your ego, but it isn't going to cause you physical harm. Nevertheless, your body will respond in the same ways as if there were a physical threat to your life: a lion in the building, a fire breaking out at your desk or a stampede at the Harvey Nichol's Boxing Day Sale.

In the heat of the moment, it can feel like life and death. It almost never is. Being wired as I am, I've found that my go-to response has typically been to fight. I can feel it rising in me, starting at my toes and working its way up to my mouth. Fight for me has always (almost always) meant using my words, rather than my fists. Whether it's been the person who's taken 'my spot' in the car park or the really senior boss whom I felt dismissed me during a meeting. My hot head usually wins out and I speak only to regret it. Almost every time. I wish I was able to keep my mouth shut, clock it, reflect on it and then decide on whether to do something about it after the event, when I could see things more clearly. I've tried to get better, only to now find that people will ask me what I'm thinking because my face clearly shows it all. If, like me, you are prone to react in the moment - here are three little questions to help ground you in those moments where you want to tear someone a new one:

- Does it need saying?
- Does it need saying now?
- Does it need saying by me?

If you answer yes to all three, then go right ahead. If not, then my advice would be to hold off. There's always time afterwards to say what needs to be said. Taking back words said in the heat of the moment? That's a bit trickier. If it's still grating on you 24 hours later, speak up within 48 hours.

Between stimulus and response, there is space. In that space is our power to choose our response. In our response lies our growth and our freedom - Viktor Frankl

KEEP THE P - PERSPECTIVE

As a human being, you are blessed with the ability to critically self-reflect. To replay situations in your head and to draw learning from them. It's all part of what it means to grow, to learn, to get older and, hopefully, wiser. The difficulty of course can come when critical reflection spirals into catastrophising and mental self-flagellation. You tell yourself all sorts of stories about a situation, most of which aren't true and before you know it, a clumsy side comment from your boss has got you looking on job websites wondering how you're going to pay the mortgage. Humans like certainty and so what tends to happen is the gaps in the story, the blanks, get filled in with your best guess. *They said that to me because they think x.* In truth, you have no idea what the person was thinking at the time; it's possible that they didn't either. The most logical solution would be to ask them, but that feels uncomfortable, so you continue to stew and fester until you either work yourself up so much that you get sick of the sound of your own voice and turn your attention elsewhere, or you're in it for the long run and it will sit with you until the next opportunity to beat yourself up unveils itself. If any of this sounds familiar to you, then here is a tool that you can use in the moment to help you regain a sense of perspective when you feel yourself spiralling. Keep it in your back pocket.

THE SCALE OF AWFULNESS

Created by Albert Ellis, the scale is designed to help you control your instinctive response to a situation and reduce your stress and anxiety levels. Here's how it goes:

1. Imagine a scale of 1-10, with 1 being the least awful and 10 being the most.
2. Now think about the worst thing that could happen to you in your life - something that would hit 10. The trick here is to recognise the worst-case scenario, but not to dwell on it.

3. Reflecting on the current challenge you are facing, what number would you give it on the scale?
4. Now ask yourself, how will you look upon this challenge differently having gained a fresh sense of perspective? What will you do/stop doing?

It's such a quick and simple way of giving yourself a reality check and regaining a sense of perspective when you feel overwhelmed. Give it a go. Trust me, it works.

Emotions are nothing more than suggestions as to how you might react. You always have a choice.

GROUNDING

When someone or something has made your blood boil and you feel yourself starting to spiral, here are some top tips for keeping your diva-like cool:

1. Stop what you are doing and take a deep breath. Inhale for four counts, hold for four counts and exhale for six counts. Doesn't that feel better already?
2. Now, let's get physical. No, I'm not talking about a workout. I mean get in touch with the

ground beneath you. If you are able, take off your shoes and socks and feel the grass or floor beneath your feet. Wiggle your toes and feel the sensation of each toe touching the ground.

3. Engage your senses. Look around and name five things you see. Listen carefully and name five things you hear. Touch something nearby and describe how it feels. Smell something and describe the scent. Taste something and savour the flavour. By engaging your senses, you bring yourself back to the present moment and out of your stressed-out mind.

4. Finally, let it go. Release that tension and negativity from your body. You can do this by imagining a balloon in front of you. Now imagine that all your stress and worry is being blown into that balloon. Watch it get bigger and feel yourself start to relax. Then, when you're ready, release it into the air and watch that shit float away.

Anger is when you're divorced from your breath long enough to focus on the things you can't control - Matt Kahn

WORK IT THROUGH

The Scale of Awfulness is a brilliant tool for working through your response in the moment. But what happens afterwards? There is learning to be gained from every situation and in that learning lies insight that will prove helpful next time similar shit goes down. It might not always feel comfortable, the outcome might be that the other person involved was being unkind, but it might also be true that you were being a little bitch about it. Awareness = Choice. Look inward, take the learning, use it to continue to build your self-awareness and allow it to assist in helping you to make a different choice next time.

We've all been there. I certainly have. I replay situations, going over and over and it can be exhausting. The downside to not reacting in the moment and having it out there and then, is that questions go unanswered until your next encounter - when you are calmer, more collected and ready to talk things through adult to adult. Knowing myself as I do, I now have a script that I work through, either in the car on the way home or in the shower as I'm washing the day off. You can either ask yourself these questions or give them to somebody else to ask you. Answer them truthfully, entertaining the mindset that behind every behaviour is a positive intent and that you might not know the whole story.

You cannot see your reflection in boiling water. Similarly, you cannot see the truth in a state of anger. When water calms, clarity comes.

1. What happened?
2. Specifically, what was it about the situation that pissed you off?
3. How much of how you are feeling is about your reaction? As opposed to what the other person said or did? Remember, nobody can make you feel a certain way. Your reaction is a choice.
4. Playing devil's advocate, if the other person was acting with positive intent, what might that be?
5. If you were being generous towards this other person, what would you say was going on for them at the time?
6. If you take yourself out of the situation, what's this issue really about?
7. If you were watching it play out on the TV, as an observer, what would you say was going on?
8. If someone you knew was experiencing this same issue, what would you advise them to do?
9. Where does this issue sit on the Scale of Awfulness, truly?
10. How likely is it that you will still be stressing about this in a week's time? How about a month?
11. How much of your precious energy are you prepared to give away to this?

WHAT A BITCH!

There will be times when you will come across somebody who you just don't vibe with. The energy is off, it might feel tricky to do work with them and maybe you aren't even sure that you trust them. You can't put your finger on it, but something doesn't feel right. Then they do something that sets your alarm bells ringing, *What a bitch! I could tell something like this was going to happen.* In that moment, it can be all too easy to tell yourself all sorts of 'truths' about what the person did or didn't do, what they were thinking at the time and what their intent was. Of course, if this thing has had a negative impact on you, the best thing to do is to have it out with them, call out their shitty behaviour and see what they have to say about it. If you aren't quite ready for that, then as uneasy as it might feel to step into their shoes (unless they are nice ones), you might just learn something that you weren't expecting. This is where changing places can help. It's helped me many times over the years and continues to provide all sorts of light bulb moments for those I work with.

The problem is almost never the problem and almost always the way you are thinking about the problem.

CHANGING PLACES

This tool helps you to explore what is going on within a particular relationship. In my experience, it works best as a physical movement exercise, but if you prefer, you can do it seated in one place. The genius of this technique is that it makes you consider a situation from three points of view:

- Your own.
- The other person's.
- That of a detached observer who knows nothing about either of you or the situation.

Here's how it goes:

Self: From your own point of view, describe what happened. What did you see, hear and feel?

Once you've spent enough time considering your side of the story, step out of your shoes and into the shoes of the other person. Do your best to embody them, try and think, speak and act as if you are them. This is where it can be helpful to change your physical position by going and sitting somewhere else or even just moving your chair to a slightly different position. When you speak, speak as if you are them in the first person e.g. *I was doing this and then Adam came in the room and...*

Other Person: From the other person's point of view, describe what happened. What was going on for you at the time? What did you see, hear and feel?

Once you've had enough of standing in their shoes, change places again. This time, taking on the role of a completely neutral third party who just so happened to be walking past at the time and saw this situation play out. They've never met either of you before and know nothing about you - they simply saw the situation for what it was.

Observer: From the position of a detached observer, describe what happened. What did you see, hear and feel?

Once you've spent the time you need to, move back to your 'Self' position.

What's different now that you've taken a multiple perspective view of the situation?

There are three sides to every story: Yours, mine and what actually happened.

CHAPTER FOURTEEN

SELF-SABOTAGE

A diva knows that the only thing standing in the way of their success, is themselves.

SELF-SABOTAGE

It was the amazing women in my life who motivated me to finally get on and write this book. They are top-tier divas. Strong women, capable women, brilliant - women. But women who, despite their talent and their obvious success - be it at home, in their personal lives or in their career, far too often got stuck inside their heads and lost sight of just how incredible they were, of their potential and the light they shine into the world. Self-doubt would show up, *I couldn't possibly do that, I'm not qualified enough.* They became more concerned with what would happen if things didn't go right, than if they did, *It's not worth the risk, can you imagine? I'd be a laughingstock.* They frequently compared their own story to that of others, *She's younger than me and look what she's got that I haven't.* Under the weight of stress and change, they downplayed their success, negating all the times when they tried and succeeded, *Well, anybody could have done that; it doesn't make me special.* Or they knew that they wanted something different for themselves, but for whatever reason, they thought it was best, or safer, to wait, *I'll wait until the kids are at school and start then; that makes more sense* - classic head over heart thinking.

This chapter is written for those women. If you recognise any of what you've heard so far in your own behaviour and you want to do something about it, then this chapter is written for you too. As I've said before, if you are fortunate enough not to have to face some of the challenges I've described, then I ask that you take these tools and principles and use them to help those around you who, at times, are their own worst enemies. Even better, gift them a copy of this book!

WHICH VOICE DO YOU LISTEN TO?

You've probably heard of the metaphor of the devil that sits on one shoulder and the angel that sits on the other. The devil tells you that you aren't good enough, that if you try then you will fail, so you might as well not bother. The angel's on the other shoulder whispering words of encouragement, telling you that you can do anything that you put your mind to. That everything you want for yourself can be found outside of your comfort zone; you just have to believe in yourself.

Which voice do you pay the most attention to? The one that says you can? Or the one that says you can't?

A bit like whipping back the curtain on the Wizard of Oz to find he's no wizard at all, the devil isn't really a devil. It isn't out to get you, to trip you up and revile in your failure. No, the devil is nothing more than a defence mechanism programmed thousands of years ago and then passed down to you through the generations. Its aim was to keep us around long enough to propagate and secure the future of the human race. Its aim, therefore, isn't to have you fail - it's to keep you alive! What's the simplest route to avoiding danger? Keep still, don't move, do nothing and stay safe. Well see here devil/wizard/programming, whatever you are - we didn't come here to stay safe; we came to win, baby.

I've said it before and I'll keep on saying it until everyone believes it - a belief is nothing more than a thought repeated. If you spend most of your time listening to the voice that says, *you can*, you will begin to believe it. You will try, and if you want it badly enough, you will succeed. If you choose, and that word is important because it is a choice, to tune into the voice which says, *you can't*, then you will do nothing. You will spend your life astride the line between your dreams and your perceived limitations.

I had a friend once who told herself that she wasn't good enough. Do you know what happened to her?

F*ck all.

Nobody is immune to self-sabotage, to the *you can't* voice. It's part of being human. We all receive the exact same outdated programming designed to protect us. So, what differentiates those who hear *you can't*, but do it anyway, and those that don't? Choice. You, dear Diva, always have a choice. The key lies in your ability to choose one thought over another.

You are faced with hundreds of decisions every day; most you won't even recognise as decisions because they are things that you've always done - habits. What to have for breakfast, what coffee to order, which supermarket to go to, etc. The thoughts which power those decisions are a critical factor in whether you choose to think positively and give stuff a go, make mistakes, learn, grow and ultimately succeed or whether you remain fixed, avoid challenges, give up easily, bitch and moan and generally be a bit of a misery tits.

Getting in your own way isn't all about the big stuff: career, relationships, goals, dreams, etc. It's often about the small stuff, the day-to-day seemingly inconsequential stuff. But this stuff adds up, right? If you tell yourself no a hundred times each day, what do you think will happen when you're offered an opportunity that scares you?

Dr Carol Dweck developed the concept of the Growth and Fixed Mindset. It goes like this:

THE GROWTH MINDSET

- Perseveres in the face of failure and sees setbacks as opportunities to learn.
- Knows that to get what you want, you have to work for it.
- Desires to learn and improve.
- Accepts criticism.

- Celebrates when others do well.
- Knows that their way isn't the only way and is open to other possibilities and 'truths'.
- Feels the fear and does it anyway.

THE FIXED MINDSET

- Avoids challenges and unfamiliar environments.
- Thinks that talent is something you're born with.
- Is defensive about criticism.
- Feels threatened when others do well.
- Thinks they know it all; there's nothing else to learn.
- Isn't open to other possibilities or versions of the truth.
- Gives up easily and thinks that when you fail, you're no good.

The growth mindset offers you the opportunity to learn, to grow and to be the person you want to be. With a fixed mindset, you have failed before you have even begun. But we don't live in a binary world; we've already talked about how we are all more than one thing, right? When Dr Carol Dweck analysed the students in her classroom, she found that whilst there were some people who sat more firmly in either one camp or the other, most people sat somewhere in the middle. The mindset that they adopted changed depending on the topic, the context and the environment. There's good news to be had here in that this middle ground offers you a choice. If you can adopt a growth mindset in one area of your life, what's stopping you from doing it in another?

- In which areas of your life do you tend to adopt a growth mindset?
- How does that change depending on what you are doing or who you are with?
- Likewise, in which areas of your life do you tend to adopt a fixed mindset?
- What are the costs to you and to others of doing so? What joys are you robbing yourself of?
- If you were to take a growth mindset approach, what would that get you that you haven't got now?

It takes ten coats of white paint to cover up just one coat of black, and yet just one coat of black to cover up ten of white. Watch how you talk to yourself. It matters.

BELIEFS

The thing that more often than not gets in the way of you living your best life, from being everything that you want to be and achieving everything you dream of, are your beliefs. Beliefs about what you are and aren't capable of, beliefs about what is and isn't possible, beliefs about anything else you can think of really.

Thoughts power beliefs, beliefs power actions, actions power outcomes, outcomes reinforce thoughts - and so the cycle continues.

If you always do what you've always done, you will always get what you've always got. It's not always easy to change beliefs, especially those that you've had for a long time. You may have even inherited them from people who held them before you, people whom you watched and learned from growing up. Beliefs are often formed through encounters with people whom we perceive to hold positions of power: parents, grandparents, teachers and bosses. They deliver a message and you believe it, because why wouldn't you? They are older than you, wiser or more senior, they must know better! Many of the beliefs that you hold about yourself will have been formed in your early years and will have involved people whom, at the time, you perceived as being superior to you in some way. Maybe a parent told you repeatedly when you were small that you were too loud. Maybe rather than taking time to support you more, your maths teacher told you to just give up because you're never going to 'get it'. Maybe your first boss told you that unless you become more confident, there's no way you're going to get promoted. This stuff sticks. And before you know it, 30 years have passed and you avoid getting over-excited because you don't want people to think you are too loud, or you don't even try to multiply in your head because you know you're no good at it, or you've stayed in the same job for so long despite being unhappy because you believe that you lack the confidence to do anything different.

Much of what we hold on to doesn't exist anymore.

A belief is nothing more than a thought repeated. The good news is that as tricky as some of these more embedded beliefs might be to change, they can be changed. Small steps repeated often and consistently will bring about different thoughts, which will bring about different actions, which bring about different outcomes, which help to affirm new beliefs.

It's not the actual words we tell ourselves that do the damage, but the meaning we attach to them. For example, if I were to insult you in a language that you didn't speak, it wouldn't mean anything to you. It wouldn't matter how loud I shouted at you, you'd still have no clue - in fact, you'd probably laugh. It's you, dear Diva, who attaches meaning to those words. Practise observing your thoughts but not believing them. In fact, when you get a 'big' thought, e.g. *I'm useless,* laugh at it as though it's gibberish - because it is.

At every moment, we always have a choice, even if it feels as if we don't. Sometimes that choice may simply be to think a more positive thought.
- Tina Turner

Whilst the technique above can be helpful in the moment, until you face up to the beliefs you carry about yourself, believing something different can prove tough. Change starts with challenging your beliefs.

Start by getting these so called beliefs out of your head and down on paper. This might be the first time you've faced some of them and seeing them in the plain harsh light of day can sometimes be enough to have you realise that some are just plain ridiculous and not worth paying any more attention to.

STEP 1: Get Them Out of Your Head: Grab some paper and write down as many beliefs that you have about yourself that hold you back, limit you and stop you from achieving what you want to, e.g.

- I'm not good enough to...
- I'm too old to...
- I'm not clever enough to...
- I don't have enough time to...

STEP 2: Interrogate Them: Take a belief and ask yourself the following:

- Is it true? What hard data and evidence do you have to back it up?
- Was it once true, but isn't anymore?
- Where did it come from? When you think about it, who's voice do you hear?
- If you knew with 100% certainty that this belief wasn't true, what would you do differently?
- Name one good reason to keep it...
- If you keep it, what's the payoff? In what way do you win?
- What would your best friend say about it?

STEP 3: Keep, Ditch or Reframe: Now ask yourself what you'd like to do with it:

- You can keep it.
- You can send that bitch packin' (throw it away).
- You can reframe it. If you were to change this belief to be more positive, empowering and/or accurate, what would it sound like instead?

Then repeat these steps for any other beliefs which you think might be holding you back. Maybe sit down with a friend and do it together. Have fun with it.

The fears we don't face become our limits.

THE POWER OF 'YET'

She's back again! Three letters and 'yet' so powerful. When things aren't going as you'd hoped and you begin to tell yourself a story like, *I can't...* or *I'm not...* drop in the word 'yet' afterwards and notice the difference that it makes. 'Yet' helps to reframe situations that aren't going well by reminding you that this isn't the end, you haven't reached the credits, this isn't the final scene and there is more to come. It provides a path to the future and can give you the confidence to carry on it. Notice the difference: *I can't do this > I can't do this, yet.* You're welcome.

Whatever the mind thinks, the thinker believes.

THE FIVE FOES OF A DIVA

OK, ready to get down to business? I present to you, and I wish I could say 'for one night only', but alas I can't - The Five Foes of a Diva. When a diva begins to doubt themselves, the culprit can often be traced back to one of these five foes. Even the most capable and inspirational of divas can find themselves at their mercy. Be wary of these devious hoes, for when they strike, they do so without warning and with ninja-like agility. Their aim is to stop you from becoming the diva that you are destined to be. They carry out their mission by feeding on your self-doubt, stimulating your mind to over-think and question even the most unquestionable, *Can I do it, really?* Have you met yourself? Of course you can! But whilst your mind is distracted chasing its own tail and tying itself up in knots, they enter and take hold. Before you know it, you're looking for the nearest exit, you're planning your leaving speech, you're tapping out of the game. You're on that midnight train to Georgia, baby and you ain't lookin' back. Sound familiar? Well, shit just got real and the game is about to change because we hold the key to stopping these foes dead in their tracks. Because like all ninjas, they operate in the dark. They need the dark to be able to move in and do their dirty work. The dark is their cloak; it's how they get close to us and make their move. Without the dark, they are nothing. Flick the light switch and what do you see? I'm interested in what you see, dear Diva. Yourself? Someone who hurt you? The scattered remains of what you once thought to be true, but know not to be anymore? Or something else? Cue some philosophical mind bending, because when I turn the lights on, I see myself. Aged four, maybe five. Unsure, frightened, wanting to stay home in the warm, in the comfort of familiarity and play with my toys. My experience leads me to believe that this is common. The 'demons' that we chastise for trying to take us down aren't demons at all. But a part of us that's trying to keep us safe, to protect us, to keep us warm, out of danger and in the comfort of familiarity.

With the knowledge and understanding of who we are and *how* we are, comes awareness. With awareness comes illumination. With illumination, the cloak is lifted and all is revealed for what it really is. Bear this in mind as we explore each of these 'foes'.

Be present as the watcher of your mind – of your thoughts and emotions as well as your reaction in various situations. Be at least as interested in your reactions as in the situation or person who causes you to react.
– Eckhart Tolle

FOE ONE: FEAR OF FAILURE

Sounds Like: *If it all goes wrong what will people think of me? They'll laugh at me; they'll know I've failed. What if x happens? I'll lose the money, what will happen to the house? OMG, what about the kids?*

If you haven't checked out the chapter titled 'Failure' yet, then this is the time to. Here are the headlines:

Failure is a construct. It exists only in the mind and is essentially our way of saying that something didn't go the way we'd expected it to. The Dali Lama is quoted as saying...

I never fail. I either win, or I learn.

Adopting the mindset that failure is an illusion cooked up for us by society, can and should become quite freeing. You can cast off the idea that if you give something a go and it doesn't work out, you haven't failed, you've learned and you will come back next time, armed with that learning, that knowledge and that insight and you will go again.

What failure really boils down to is the expectations that you place on yourself. The idea that you have one chance and one chance only to get things right and if things don't go to plan, then you've failed; you are 'a failure'. But you don't stop there. You then self-flagellate by allowing this one episode to define your entire existence, attaching all sorts of untruths to yourself, *I'll never make it work, I'm not good/clever enough, I shouldn't have even tried, I'm not worthy of this anyway, I'll just go back to what I know.*

Bullshit. I'll say it again, failure is a construct. Whether you buy into it or not is down to one person, YOU. You can take the growth mindset approach and put it down to learning, or you can take the fixed mindset approach and wallow in self-pity. If you choose the latter, know that a) this behaviour is not befitting of a diva, and b) you won't be much fun to be around and nobody likes a misery tits. Instead, say to yourself, *Well that didn't go how I'd expected.* Then dust yourself off, stand up straight, fix your lippy and go again.

It's perfectly normal to feel a sense of fear about failure. In fact, it's estimated that almost half of us would say that fear of failure is the biggest roadblock to achieving our goals. Remember what we talked about in the chapter on 'Confidence'? Your brain is designed to protect you, to keep you safe from perceived dangers and threats to your life. But most of the time, we aren't dealing with life and death. What's the worst that could possibly happen if you were to give something a go and it didn't work out? Death? Hardly.

It can be helpful to acknowledge the signals that your brain and body are giving you. I'll often say something to myself like, *OK I hear you, but we're alright. This isn't life and death, you can pipe down and let me enjoy this moment.* A bit like a noisy toddler at your heels seeking attention, once you acknowledge them and let them say their piece, they're happy to go off and leave you alone for a bit - the same is true when it comes to the messages your brain sends you.

Think like a queen. A queen is not afraid to fail. Failure is another steppingstone to greatness - Oprah Winfrey

FOE ONE A: CATASTROPHISING

When does fear of failure tip into the realms of catastrophising? If you haven't come across this term before, then catastrophising is described as a tendency to exaggerate the negative. A person who is prone to catastrophising might seek out every possible negative consequence of their actions and blow even the most seemingly neutral of decisions way out of proportion. Catastrophising isn't always about worrying about the future though. Often people who catastrophise spend time ruminating on past experiences and how these might return to haunt them someday. Generally, catastrophising is fuelled not by data and evidence, but by assumption. This can easily cause people to spiral out of control and become overwhelmed by decisions they need to make. Naming and then challenging these thoughts can be a helpful starting place. Sometimes saying them aloud to a friend or writing them down can be enough for the person to see these thoughts for what they are. Doing work around beliefs and seeking out hard evidence and data to support the belief is also a helpful next step. But catastrophising isn't just about having a generally negative disposition. Sometimes these thoughts can be associated with physical pain in the body - that's how strongly they are felt. For this reason, if any of what you've heard so far is chiming with you and you're concerned that your catastrophising is having a negative impact on your quality of life, then I encourage you to speak to a professional about it. Know that you aren't alone, it's not just you. With the right support, through coaching or therapy, it can be managed to the point where it isn't affecting your daily life.

FEAR = Future Events Appearing Real.

FOE ONE B: FEAR OF SUCCESS

What are you afraid might happen if you try and you succeed?

You might find this an interesting question to pause on. So often we focus on what would happen if things didn't go the way we wanted. But what if you were to set your sights, aim and achieve this thing that you desire? Then what? The space outside your comfort zone can, if you allow it, appear scary. It's change and with change, even uber-positive change, comes loss.

- Loss of life as you know it.
- Loss of the familiar.
- Loss of the thrill of the chase (because you've achieved it).
- If your goal is career-related, then loss of not seeing current colleagues every day.
- If your goal is relationship orientated, then loss of certain people in your life, who, whilst you know aren't good for you, won't be there anymore.
- Loss of your current daily routine.
- Loss of your sense of identity. *If I achieve this thing, how might it change me?*

Ask yourself, what is really holding you back? Fear of trying and failing? Or fear of trying and getting everything you've ever dreamed of?

Whether it's fear of being able to sustain what you've achieved, fear of leaving people behind, fear of losing yourself, fear of your success opening you up to criticism, or fear of making lots of money and not knowing how to manage it - if you are living in the future, you are hallucinating. That shit's not real, it hasn't happened and if I were your friend, I'd be saying that the fact you are thinking about this stuff now before it's happened, shows me that you are committed to making sure it doesn't happen. It's those who throw themselves headfirst into success without stopping to think about the consequences that need to be worried, dear Diva - not you. So, write this stuff down, get it out of your head and onto paper. Look at it for what it is and then think about what you are willing to say, *so long* to and what (and who) you aren't. Then get to work.

May your choices reflect your hopes, not your fears - Nelson Mandela

FOE TWO: COMPARING YOURSELF TO OTHERS

Sounds Like: *They're so much better than me, look what they've got that I haven't, I'm not half as successful as they are, I wish I had what they have (money/house/ car, etc).*

Appearances are deceiving and what's more, in today's world of social media, influencers and filters, appearances are in fact designed to be deceiving. What we see online isn't real - it's made up. It's designed to sell a person, a product or a dream. I'd forgive you for falling for it because I know that I have. Avoid falling into the trap of this fateful foe, because no good can come from it.

When it comes to what you see online, take it with a pinch of salt, or even better, treat it all as panto. Laugh at it because it's laughable. It's not real.

When you think about the people you know (or think that you know), I need you to hear this - you only ever see the bits of people that they want you to see. The achievements they share, the house, the car, the white picket fence, the baby in designer clothes and the perfect little doggy sat obediently. You don't see what's going on behind the scenes and believe me when I say there is always more than meets the eye;

health challenges, relationship problems, financial issues, you name it. These problems and no doubt many more are present in households up and down your street, perhaps even your own. How many famous people who appeared on the outside to have it all, have died through suicide because they were fighting a battle behind closed doors? Too many.

You have no idea what price people have paid to get where they are and to have the things they have. That beautiful home? It was paid for by the inheritance they received when they lost both their parents. That wealthy husband? They went through two abusive relationships until they met Mr Right. That perfect little baby? It took three rounds of IVF and two miscarriages to start their family. That amazing job that 'fell into their lap'? They sacrificed time with their family so that they could go back to night school and get the grades they needed.

When you find yourself comparing where you are in life with where you think others are - stop. No good can come from here. Focus only on what you can control: your story, your journey, your life.

If you really knew the price people have paid for what they have, would you walk their path? My bets on no.

The topic of money, or the appearance of it, is an area of life about which I often hear people comparing themselves. It's all too easy to see somebody out and about dressed in designer labels, with expensive looking jewellery and a designer bag and to think, *Oh gosh, they must be loaded! How did they manage that? I wish I could be like them.* Well, this might be news to you, but beware people who wear their money, who dress in designer clothes and appear to take expensive looking Instagram holidays. Because people who have money (real money) do not 'wear' it. It's true, honest. Wealthy people do not wear their money. They look just like you and me, normal, ordinary. In fact, I dare say that some of the wealthiest people I've met have been amongst the scruffiest, because who do they have to impress? They've got millions in the bank, they can dress how they damn well please - and often it's scruffy shirts, worn-out shorts and sandals dating back to the time BC. Some of my dearest friends are 'of money'. They are wealthy, some of them rich, some super-rich and yet you would walk past them without giving them a second look. They look just like my old mate Sue, who works the checkout at Tesco. Yet you compare yourself to the person who on the surface looks like they have money, when in fact they're so far in the red that they're eating beans on toast three times a day and selling the designer bags they bought last week on credit to pay their bills. If you are going to compare yourself to anybody, which of course I advise against - but if you were to insist, then compare yourself to Sue. She didn't grow up with much; she wasn't from a wealthy family. She got a bit of money when her Mum died, which she didn't spend, she invested. She saw the bigger picture and she played the long game. She lives well below her means and now that investment has meant that she never needs to work again. But she does, because she likes talking to people and it gets her out of the house. Next time you see her, say hi. If she's not working the tills at Tesco, she'll be standing behind you in a queue somewhere, yet you'd have no idea she's there.

Always be a first-rate version of yourself, instead of a second-rate version of somebody else
- Judy Garland

FOE THREE: FEELING LIKE AN IMPOSTER

Sounds Like: *It was luck that got me here; any minute they'll figure me out. I'm a fraud; I'm not as qualified as these other people are.*

If you knew that everyone in the room felt the same as you, what difference would it make? There is an important point behind this question - ready for it? Anybody worth comparing yourself to will feel this exact same way at some point in their life. Some more frequently than others, granted, but they will. I've worked with people from all walks of life, from people who sweep factory floors to CEOs of major global companies. Do you want to know the thing that each of them had in common? It's that at times in their life, not just their career, they felt like an imposter. They questioned their position, how they got there and whether they were worthy of it. They compared themselves to their colleagues, telling themselves all sorts of stories about who was more or less qualified, and they generally made their tenure miserable. It was only afterwards, with the benefit of hindsight that they were able to look back and see what they were doing to themselves.

What interested me was the way in which they chose to disclose these feelings. They appeared to feel shame and embarrassed at sharing how they felt. To them, it was akin to making an admission to a parent or teacher. It was visceral. They made themselves appear smaller in their chair, they found it difficult to meet my gaze and they appeared to feel pain in disclosing how they really felt. Let me tell you, when you've sat across from a CEO whose business is worth millions and whose personal wealth is that region too, and you watch as they pour their heart out, in floods of tears about the fact they don't know how they got to where they are and that each of their team is, according to them, 'far more qualified', 'inspiring' and 'business-like' than they are - you gain a new perspective on this stuff. For this reason, I abhor the term 'imposter syndrome' because it isn't a syndrome at all. A syndrome implies something you either have or don't have - you are either afflicted or not. You either test negative or positive. The reality as far as I'm concerned, is that we *all* experience what I prefer to term 'imposterism' from time to time and in all areas of our lives, not just our work. For example, *OMG, why did they choose me? They are so much hotter than I am; surely they'd be better off dating someone who looks more like them.* Pay attention as I tell you that it's all a load of bollocks.

Going back to my example about the CEO and countless others, how do you think I responded to their 'disclosure'? Guess. I laughed. *Is that it? Is that the thing you've been agonising over telling me?* Now I didn't reply in that way to cause more embarrassment or shame but to make a firm and clear point. Feeling out of our depth or feeling the urge to compare our success or achievements to others is not only futile, but it's a given - it comes with the territory. Rather than allowing it to live in the dark, as a taboo, something not to be admitted to anybody at any cost, bring it into the light. Hold it up in the cold harsh light of day as something not to be afraid or ashamed of, but rather as just another facet of being human. Of life. Of existence. It's panto. It's laughable. So laugh at it. Don't allow it to fester, to take root. Doing so will only commit you to a life of internal agony and untapped dreams. Don't let that bitch win.

If your imposterism has reached the point where it's affecting the quality of your life, then talk to somebody about it. A friend, a therapist or a coach. The more you let it air, the lighter its grip becomes.

The moment we realise that we are all dealing with the same shit and just doing our best to Get by - we are freed.

FOE FOUR: DOWNPLAYING YOUR SUCCESSES AND TALENTS

Sounds Like: *Yeah, but everyone can do that; it doesn't make me special. I was just in the right place at the right time.*

There's an activity I like to use as a way of starting team coaching sessions, it's called 'What have you got going for you?' It's simple. All the group has to do is list as many things as possible that they, well, have going for them: achievements, successes, skills, talents, kids, pets, difficulties overcome, anything and everything from passing their driving test to climbing Mount Kilimanjaro and every primary school accolade and well done from their dentist for having no fillings, in between. Its simplicity is deceiving, because in digging deep, not only do people remind themselves of successes long forgotten, but the activity also causes them to reframe past events as successes,

Now I think about it, getting to grade three on the recorder at nine years old was a success, wasn't it? People realise that no, not everybody is a black belt in karate and no, not everyone has kicked cancer's ass. So why do we so often shrug off our achievements on the basis that 'everyone' must have done that?

Maybe it's to not appear arrogant or boastful? The problem here is that arrogance stems less from sharing our achievements and more from failing to acknowledge our weaknesses. We should feel good about the things we've achieved and talk about our strengths positively, without seeing it as arrogance - unless you're a knobhead, then don't bother and if you just questioned whether you are in fact a knobhead, you passed the test - you're not.

Is it because we've been programmed to downplay our talents? By that I mean, as a child were you led to believe that nothing you did was good enough? If that's the case, then just know that it's not true. Whatever went on back then had absolutely nothing to do with you and absolutely everything to do with the adults involved. If you want to figure out what's going on there, then take a look at the sub-chapter on 'Beliefs' in the chapter titled 'Knowing Yourself'.

Is it because we're afraid of how people might treat us differently? That they might think we're getting too big for our boots? This is an easy one. STOP. No good can come from here. If you haven't realised already, you can't control what other people think. They will think what they want to think, which generally means they are more focused on what's going on for them, than what's going on for you. The bitches out there will talk regardless of whether you say anything or not. You might as well give them something good to talk about. And here's one of the best pieces of advice I was ever given - if you knew how often people deal with their own shit by projecting it onto other people, you would learn to take almost nothing personally.

Is it because we lack self-esteem? Do we prefer to focus on other people's achievements to compensate for our own lack of self-esteem, and find happiness in making them feel good about themselves because we aren't able to do the same for ourselves? If this sounds like you, then take a look at the chapter titled 'Standing Up For Yourself'.

In truth, it could be any, all or none of the above. Only you really know why you do it. My advice? Remember that the world isn't binary; you can be, and indeed are, more than one thing, dear Diva. You can be kind and gracious and caring and compassionate, and you can know you're the shit. Ain't it a beautiful world we live in?

In the end they will judge you anyway - so do what you damn well please.

FOE FIVE: PUTTING OFF UNTIL YOU'RE 'READY'

Sounds like: *I'll wait until next year, 'till the kids are at school or maybe 'till I've lost some weight. Thinking about it, it makes sense to wait until we've moved house, when things are a bit more stable. I'll do it then.*

Sound familiar? This is an interesting one because it causes us to tap into our logic, our 'head brain' (as opposed to our heart or gut). It's easy to find logical reasons for why you'd be better off waiting when you go looking for them. Don't be fooled into allowing reasoning to trick you into thinking you've made an informed decision, and that informed = better. Informed is only ever informed when you listen to all three of your brains: Head (logic and reasoning), Heart (dreams and desires) and Gut (instinct and intuition). Invite all three to the party before making a decision. See the chapter titled 'Getting Shit Done' for more on decision making.

What's really behind the postponement? Is it fear? Fear of what? Fear of failure, of getting it wrong and people poking fun? Or fear of success, of getting it right and of things being different? For a long time, I got in my own way and put off doing the things I wanted because I was afraid of it going wrong and of the things that people would say.

What I've come to realise is that I don't give a shit what people have to say about me, because...

- If they are talking about me then they are giving someone else a break - and I can handle being talked about.
- My ego says, *Yeah, go on, talk about me, because I'm worth talking about.*
- It's all just panto anyway. We can't take any of it too seriously or we'll end up miserable.

So it was never really failure I was afraid of at all; it was success. I was, and to a degree still am, afraid of what will happen if I achieve the things I want and then things change. Take this book as an example. What if people read what I have to say and then themselves have something to say about it? Will I need to put photographs of myself on my social media to sell the book? *Oh god - cringe.* Will I need to visit places that I haven't been to before? Will I still be able to get home on time to take care of the dogs? But of course, it's all nonsense because it hasn't happened yet - and as I like to say:

If you're living in the past or the future, then you're hallucinating.

Go with the flow. Focus on the process, not the product and all will be worked out in time.

Maybe you consider yourself a perfectionist? *If a job's worth doing, it's worth doing well and if I can't do it exactly how I want to, then I'm better off waiting until I can.* My view is that perfectionism devours progress. It eats it up. Rather than waiting until the conditions are just right before starting, just start somewhere. You can build from there and eventually make it look like the image you have in your mind, but you have to start somewhere. Most of the biggest, most recognisable brands in the world started out with a shitty logo, no website, no grand vision or strategy - just a passion for their product and a lot of grit and determination. I'm a big believer in 'done' being better than 'perfect'. JFDI (Just F*cking Do It).

But for you, perhaps it isn't about fear or perfectionism. Maybe it's about a need to put other people's needs above your own? Maybe you are so focused on making sure that first and foremost other people get what they need, that you place your own wants, needs and desires on the back burner? Making sure that the kid's routine isn't disturbed and that they have stability. Making sure that you aren't putting extra pressure on your partner to pick up any slack that you would have otherwise picked up. Not wanting to burden elderly relatives by asking them to help with the school run while you are off 'indulging your fantasies'. Whilst I commend your caring and compassionate nature, I wouldn't be doing my job if I didn't help you to consider the flip side:

- What if the kids would enjoy things being mixed up a bit every now and then? What if seeing their parent doing something that makes them truly happy inspires them to do the same one day?
- What if your partner is just chomping at the bit to step it up and create some more space for you to achieve your dreams? What if in doing so, they see that as their little contribution towards your success?
- What if those elderly relatives are feeling low, and spending time with your kids makes them feel young again?

Of course, the first thing to do is to ask. If you don't ask, you don't know - you're working in the dark and telling yourself stories. Ask and all will be revealed.

What is the price you pay for martyrdom, dear Diva? And is it worth it?

There's never a good time. There will always be reasons to wait and to go later - especially if you go looking for them. All we ever really have is this moment - the present. Start somewhere and start now.

FOE FIVE A: PROCRASTINATING

Procrastinating is delaying something which is important by focusing instead on less important, but potentially more interesting tasks. There are countless articles online about procrastination with hundreds, if not thousands, of procrastination-beating tips and strategies. I'm going to opt for telling you a story instead. I first drafted this book in 2020 using a flipchart and post-it notes - it looked lovely. I'd planned out each chapter, under which I'd planned each of the sub-chapters - and I was proud of it. I got so excited at the prospect that one day I could be an author and I told everyone who would listen about my plans. What happened next? Nothing. Sweet FA. I came up with every excuse in the book as to why I was better off focussing on other tasks instead of getting on and writing the book. From research to designing the cover, parking the web domains, setting up the social media accounts, planning the guest list for the launch - all the fun and far more interesting stuff, everything except writing the book. What followed was a period marked by guilt at not having done this thing that I wanted, embarrassment that I'd told everyone it was coming but hadn't even started and self-flagellation over why I was seemingly incapable of making any progress. It wasn't until recently that all was made clear to me. It took me leaving my job in corporate, where I'd been for 16 years, to start to discover who I really was - beneath the business-like persona. Who I found was someone who was bright and colourful, playful and sarcastic, someone who was so much more creative than I'd ever realised and who was on a mission to help people feel good about themselves. When I looked back at the original book draft, it all made sense. It was boring. It was serious. It was trying to be what so many other books in its genre were. It was dull, and most importantly - it wasn't me. What happened next was a process of re-invention. It was no longer a book for businesspeople; it was a book for my best friend - for the world. It was no longer serious and academic, full of references. It was playful, provocative and, wait for it...it had swear words in it! I fell in love with it because it felt like the only book that I could write. It was me through and through. And what happened? When I sat down to write, it flowed. The words came easily.

What's my point? If you are putting off this thing that you supposedly want so much, perhaps you don't want it as much as you think you do. Ask yourself:

- How much do I want it, really?
- What would make me want it more?

We only get one go, dear Diva. Don't look back in 20/30 years with regret that you were the only thing standing in your way. Instead, look back knowing that you gave it your best shot.

GIVE YOUR FANS WHAT THEY WANT

We end this chapter with a mind bending thought. This is a bit out there, but stick with me...

Remember the movie The Truman Show?

Well, imagine for a moment that the people around you are all paid actors and that without realising it, you have been playing the lead role in the movie of your life.

Behind the scenes, the entire cast and all the viewers are rooting for you, cheering you on, just longing for you to get out of your own head, realise your brilliance and achieve all the things that you desire.

It's time to give the fans what they want, dear Diva.

Mic drop.

CHAPTER FIFTEEN

WORRYING

A diva knows that they suffer more in their imagination than in real life.

WORRYING

It's been estimated that we spend an average of 1 hour and 50 minutes per day worrying. Over an average lifespan of 73 years, that adds up to a staggering 5 years and 3 months of our lives spent fretting over the big stuff, the small stuff and everything in between. Think for a second about what's changed in your life over the past 5 years: the things you've achieved, the places you've been, the people you've met, the joy you've experienced. Now imagine that you'd saved up all your worry, meaning that none of it had happened. I mean, you might be pleased that some of it hadn't happened - but stick with the good stuff for a minute. Gone, wiped out - eradicated. Not by some Men in Black style memory wiping device, but by your own hand. You allowed your self-prescribed, self-induced and self-inflicted worry and fear to keep you from achieving the things you wanted, from visiting the places you desired, from meeting the people that you were destined to meet and from experiencing the joy that the universe had lined up for you. How does it feel? Shit? Good, it should. In some ways, we'd be better off saving up all our worry and spending it all at once, at least that way it's over and done with and we can get on with our lives knowing that it won't get in our way. The reality should give us more reason for concern because we can't save it all up to use in one go. Instead, it's there with us every day. We never know when it's going to show up and how it might affect us.

You've heard me say this before: Thought = Action = Result. It makes sense then that how we think about a situation will determine the outcome we experience.

If you find that your worrying is going into overdrive and is taking over your life, then take a look at the chapter titled 'Self-Sabotage', specifically the Five Foes of a Diva - Catastrophising.

99% of the things that we worry about never happen. I stand by that. And yet we willingly enter into this game of cat and mouse with ourselves, worrying about stuff that is almost never going to happen. Nobody is immune to worry, not even a diva. When worry shows its face, the question I go to first is - can I do something about this situation? If the answer is *yes,* then I will. If the answer is *no,* it's out of my control, then I have a choice to make. I can accept that I can't do anything about it and go about my business, or I can let it fester until such point as it becomes something I can control, or I tire myself out with unnecessary and pointless worry.

Don't use your precious energy to worry. Use it to believe that things will be OK.

When you find yourself worrying, there's a well-known mantra that can help:

Grant me the serenity to accept the things I cannot change, the courage to change the things I can, and the wisdom to know the difference.
- The Serenity Prayer by Reinhold Niebuhr

YOU CAN'T CONTROL EVERYTHING

Just as not every battle is yours to fight, not every worry is yours to hold. If you're used to being in control, if you like to help people or if you are a prolific worrier, for example, you are worrying about whether Jill, who works in your local bakery, is going to find a babysitter next Tuesday because she mentioned in passing that it's her birthday and she didn't have anyone to have the kids (true story), then picking up other people's worries might come more naturally to you than to others. Try as you may, dear Diva, you can't do it all.

I remember a conversation I had with a past colleague of mine when she joined the team I was in at the time. She'd come to me with a project plan for how she wanted to spend her first six months and wanted to talk it through with me before she presented it to the HR Director. As she started talking, more and more bits of paper came out of her folder. Just when I thought we'd reached the end, she pulled out more. Before we knew it, the entire table was covered in sheets of paper. She was a big-picture thinker; she thought broad and wide. She saw connections and interdependencies that just didn't occur to me. She was smart; she could see what needed to be done and come hell or high water she was going to get it done. The challenge was that what she'd presented to me wasn't her plan for the next six months at all, it was way more than that. It was a plan for the entire HR function. And in truth, it was more like a plan for the next three years! More than half of the stuff on that table wasn't even hers to own, but she could see that it needed doing and that nobody else was doing it. I remember looking at her and drawing her attention to all these bits of paper laid out in front of her. As beautiful and well-considered as each was, there was no way she was going to be able to do it in six months, even if there were ten of her.

The paper analogy is one I've used a lot since. It can be all too easy to go around picking up other people's bits of paper and adding them to your own stash, especially if you are results driven - or you lack the boundaries needed to say, *No, that's your shit, not mine - you do it.* What would happen if you were to go from place to place picking up tasks and worries that don't belong to you? What good is carrying around other people's stuff? You can't do anything with it; it isn't yours. All that will happen is the load will become greater and greater until it weighs so heavy that something has to give.

Here's a simple question for you.

Right now, what are you owning that isn't yours to own?

- Other people's happiness?
- Other people's problems?
- Other people's worries and concerns?

STOP

Whatever you are owning that isn't yours to own – put that shit down, it doesn't belong to you.

CIRCLE OF CONTROL

The circle of control is a simple tool for identifying what you can and can't control in any given situation. Imagine three circles, one inside the other.

Circle of Control (Innermost Circle): These are the things that you have full control over. E.g. your goals, your priorities, your boundaries, your choices, your reactions, your self-talk and your self-care.

Circle of Influence (Middle Circle): These are things which you may be able to influence but can't fully control. E.g. Your job, your relationships, your family, your reputation, the behaviours of others.

Circle of Concern (Outer Circle): These things are outside of your control. There's nothing you can do about them, so let that shit go. Don't lose any more sleep over it. E.g. the news, the economy, the weather, war, how people choose to interpret your words and actions, what other people think of you and...wait for it - the past!

If you find yourself worrying about something, ask yourself:

- Can I control it?
- Can I influence it?
- Or is this something bigger than me?

If you can't control it, don't stress about it. If you can't influence it in some way, don't lose sleep over it. Worrying about things that are beyond your control is pointless. Don't give it any more of your precious time, dear Diva. Focus only on what you can change, not what you can't.

Worrying doesn't take away tomorrow's problems - but it does take away today's peace.

AVOID FILLING IN THE GAPS

When dealing with human beings, you have to accept that you will never really know what's going on for somebody. Even the people involved won't have all the answers. Unless you've developed a knack for mind reading, you have to accept that there are always unknowns. You might not like it, but that's the truth. Ruminating on things like:

- What did they mean when they said that?
- What was their intent there?
- Were they trying to be helpful? Or were they being bitchy?
- Were they thinking x about me?

STOP.

There is no point trying to fill in the gaps - you will only get it wrong and risk winding yourself up while doing it. Why do it to yourself? You're better than that, come on. If someone has annoyed you, the best thing to do, once you've calmed down, is to talk to them about it. Take a look at the chapters titled 'Keeping Your Cool' and 'Standing Up For Yourself' for some strategies and tools that will help you 'de-hulk' and deal with the situation as the diva that you are.

When you notice yourself filling in the gaps and jumping to all sorts of conclusions, I have a surefire way of stopping you in your tracks. It might even be enough to avoid you having to take any further action to find out what was really going on. It's a simple question that I often ask myself...

WHAT AM I MAKING THIS MEAN?

If I could surround this question with golden light and have confetti cannons exploding behind it, then I would. It's that bloomin' fabulous. Believe me, this question has kept me out of a whole lot of trouble and has saved me hours, days even, of time spent worrying. I think it's so effective at defusing a situation for a few reasons:

- It implies accountability, 'What am I making this mean?'
- It reinforces the idea that you are always at choice. You could make it mean x, or actually, you could make it mean something else, something more helpful.
- It reminds you that the world isn't black and white, everything is open to interpretation and there is always more going on than meets the eye.

This is my gift to you, dear Diva - try it. The next time you're worrying about something someone said to you, ask yourself:

- What am I making this mean?
- Is that true? Says who? What evidence do I have?
- What if another story were true, a more helpful one? What might that be?
- How much of a shit do I really give about this?

NOBODY CARES

It might sound harsh, but it's true. Nobody is thinking about you in the way that you are thinking about yourself. Everyone is way too wrapped up in their own stuff to care on any meaningful level - with the exception of your loved ones, of course. If you're worrying about what people are thinking about you, or you're ruminating on how people might interpret something you said - STOP:

- What people think about you is none of your damn business. Get your nose out of where it doesn't belong. They will think what they want to, whether you worry or not. Remember: If you knew how often people deal with their shit by projecting it onto others, you would learn to take almost nothing personally.
- Trust that if what you said has bothered somebody, they will come to you to talk about it. If they don't, it's nothing to worry about. You're good. Crack on.

The concept that 'nobody cares' was a big awakening for me. The idea that nobody is thinking about you the way you're thinking about you was a concept that really set me free - Dan Levy

KEEP THAT PERSPECTIVE, BABY

With so much going on in the world and with our lives becoming increasingly busier, things can sometimes seem worse than they are. Especially under the weight of stress, strain and overwhelm, otherwise small, inconsequential things can blow up in an instant. Suddenly you find that you're spending so much of your time and attention on something that in the greater scheme of things doesn't really matter that much.

When you find yourself blowing things out of proportion, give these activities a try and experience how they will help you regain perspective and re-direct your focus towards the things that are more worthy of a diva's time and attention.

Scale of Awfulness: It's so good that I've brought it back again. You will also find this tool in the chapter titled 'Keeping Your Cool'.

1. Imagine a scale of 1-10, with 1 being the least awful and 10 being the most.
2. Now think about the worst thing that could happen to you in your life - something that would hit 10. The trick here is to recognise the worst-case scenario, but not to dwell on it.
3. Reflecting on the current challenge you are facing, what number would you give it on the scale?

4. Now ask yourself, how will you look upon this challenge differently having gained a fresh sense of perspective? What will you do/stop doing?

It's such a quick and simple way of giving yourself a reality check and regaining a sense of perspective when you feel overwhelmed. Give it a go. Trust me, it works.

Emotions are nothing more than suggestions as to how you might react. You always have a choice.

Zoom Out: This is a strategy that I swear by if I notice myself start to feel big emotions about relatively small things. It's simple, here's how it works:

1. Take out your smartphone and open the Google Earth app. If you don't have it, you can download it for free.
2. Zoom right in on your location, your house or wherever you are and say aloud the thing that's worrying you.
3. Now start to slowly zoom out, revealing the other houses on your street. Ask yourself what you think the people living in those houses might be experiencing at this very moment. What worries might they have? They might

have money worries, they might have worries about their health. They might be battling illness. They might be caring for loved ones. They might be struggling to feed their family. They might be doing everything possible not to fall apart.

4. As you continue to zoom out, revealing your town, your city, your county, your country, your continent and eventually the beautiful blue and green planet that we call home, ask yourself, in the grand scheme of what's going on in the world, how important is this thing I'm worrying about, really?

You're welcome.

When something is making you worry, ask yourself: Will this still matter to me tomorrow? How about next week? What about in a month's time? A year? If the answer is no, don't waste one more second of your precious time.

CHUCK IT IN YOUR F*CK-IT BUCKET

So, you've given some of the activities above a go and hopefully you're now feeling better than you were before; great. But maybe despite having detached yourself from this worry, you're still left carrying it around, unsure where or how to put it down. This next technique is a mash-up of two ideas courtesy of my darling mummy. It goes like this...

- First, imagine your very own f*ck-it bucket at the opposite end of the room to you - it can be any colour you like.
- Now imagine the worry you've been carrying as a piece of paper in your hands.
- Screw the piece of paper up as tightly as you can. As you do this, visualise all of the worry and anxiety leaving your body and being trapped inside this tightly screwed-up ball.
- When you are ready, launch the ball of paper as hard as you can in the direction of your f*ck-it bucket and watch it slam-dunk.
- Then, don't give it another thought...flick your hair and walk away.

Credit: Jane, Adam's Mum

CHAPTER SIXTEEN

TAKING CARE OF YOURSELF

A diva knows that everything works better after it's been unplugged for a while.

SLOW DOWN TO GO FASTER

Now listen up. As a diva, your greatest asset is yourself. Your body is the vehicle by which you do good in the world. It's through your body that you shine light into the lives of others. Taking care of yourself should be high on your list of priorities. If it isn't, then you should ask yourself why. Too busy? Other seemingly more important things to do? Not enough hours in the day? Now before I call bullshit on you, maybe you've got the wrong end of the stick. Self-care doesn't have to take hours. It's not about going to the gym every day, contorting yourself into all sorts of suggestive yoga poses or meditating at dawn. What self-care really comes down to is saying to yourself - *I matter too* and saying that through small actions that make you feel more like yourself, that replenish and rejuvenate you. Five minutes sat in the garden with a cup of tea listening to the birds, a hot bubble bath after a long day, picking yourself up a little treat when you are doing the big shop. Just small things that make you stop, smile and feel a little more grounded. You will not, I repeat not, hear me telling you what you should or shouldn't eat, or that you need to move more. This isn't that kind of book!

Our lives are getting busier and busier. Technology designed to make our lives easier; email, WhatsApp, smart speakers, smartphones, etc, just create space to be filled by even more 'stuff'. How many WhatsApp groups are you part of? How many times does your phone ping a day? How many meetings get squeezed into your diary without any space in between? Of course, since more meetings are now online, you don't even get the opportunity to run to your next appointment, you just sit staring at a screen as one face disappears and another one pops up - grim.

Life is full. Therefore, you are likely full too. When you are full, you can easily lose touch with yourself. Your energy becomes focused on what's happening outside of your body and you miss what's going on inside. Your body will tell you what you need at every moment of every day. To eat, to drink, to rest, to sleep, to move, to be still, to seek the company of others. Listen and it will speak. I hope that some of the ideas in this chapter help you to create a bit more space in your day for stillness, for joy and for replenishing your mind, heart, body and soul. Know that this isn't a set menu, but more a buffet of ideas. You choose which items to pick up and which to walk by. Keeping with the food metaphor, if you haven't already, you will discover, in time, your own cocktail of habits and strategies to take care of yourself. In the meantime, allow mine to whet your appetite.

If you're living life at 90mph, even the most beautiful moments will be nothing but a blur. Slow down and take in the view.

'SCHNAPP OUT OF IT' - CHER

Who doesn't love a quiz? Let's begin by getting a clearer picture of what's going on when it comes to how you take care of yourself. Answer honestly, go with your gut and try not to overthink it. Also, no blame no shame - it is what it is.

To what degree are you experiencing the following...	Not at all	Sometimes	Frequently	Consistently
Regularly skipping meals				
Feeling stressed or overwhelmed				
Not getting enough sleep				
Ignoring the signals your body is giving you (aches/pains/stress etc)				
Taking on too much				
Saying *yes* when you want to say *no*				
Not taking enough 'me' time				
Avoiding asking for help				
Worrying about things you can't control				
Spending too much time on social media				

Talking unkindly to yourself				
Holding your breath when stressed				
Feeling bad about your eating habits				
Not making time to move your body				
Not using all of your annual leave at work				
Working long hours without proper breaks				
Not asking yourself what you're thinking or feeling				
Focussing more on work than on other areas of life				
Not making time for hobbies				

What do you notice about your results? Any surprises?

If most of your scores were in the frequently or consistently columns, then it's Whoopi time again because, 'You in danger, girl'.

Everyone has off-days, that's normal. But if you are treating yourself this way most of the time? Well, something needs to change. There's nothing to feel bad about; yesterday is in the past and as I like to say...

If you've got one leg in the past and another in the future, you're pissing on the present.

You have a choice from here, dear Diva. Take small, manageable steps that remind yourself just a little bit more each day that you matter. Because you matter a lot. To me and to those around you. So sort yourself out.

Oh, and for those of you who scored more towards the left side, good for you. Keep an eye on your habits and make sure you don't allow them to drift for too long. Your light shines from inside. Keep it burning bright, baby.

'ALMA, CHECK YOUR BATTERY' - SISTER ACT

Despite your body being made from universal energy that's billions of years old, you don't have an endless supply of the stuff. Think of yourself as having a built-in battery. You wake up in the morning and provided you've had a decent night's sleep, your battery is fully charged and you are bright-eyed and bushy-tailed, just rearing to get out there and let the world have it. As soon as you walk out the door your battery starts to deplete. As the day goes on and your battery gets lower and lower, you get slower and things take a bit longer to process, the odd app crashes until bedtime comes and it's time for a recharge.

Your body will be giving you signs throughout the day, warning you how much battery you have left. But if you aren't used to listening out for those signs, you might not hear them.

Just as your phone battery can be depleted by running an app that uses lots of processing power, so can your own internal battery. Fortunately, just as certain tasks (or people) can cause your energy to drain, others can top it up and give you a boost, a bit like plugging your phone in to charge throughout the day.

- What or who tops up your battery?
- What or who drains it?

Self-care shouldn't have to come out of an imminent need for relief when everything comes tumbling down. It should be deliberate, it should be scheduled, it should become a habit.
- Oprah Winfrey

MANAGE YOUR PRECIOUS ENERGY

It's your energy, not your time that is your greatest asset, dear Diva. Your energy is unique to you; it is precious and should be spent wisely.

Think of yourself as having four core energies. They swirl around inside of you, glowing brightly when they are replenished and fading as they are depleted. It is your job to manage these energies, keeping them burning bright so that you can draw from them where needed, to help yourself and to support others in need.

Here they are:

Mind Energy: This is the energy associated with thinking. It deals with logic, analysis, rationality and reasoning. It drives curiosity, focus and planning. Watch out though, too much of it can hinder passion, enthusiasm and creativity - so called 'head over heart' mentality.

Body Energy: This is the energy associated with physical health and wellbeing, which also contributes towards getting things done. This body energy helps to maintain concentration and stamina in order to follow through with your commitments. You will notice this energy most when it is depleting. You will feel tired and perhaps stressed. Body energy can be replenished through getting a good night's sleep, rest, a nourishing diet and exercise.

Heart Energy: This is the energy associated with emotions, connection and relationships. This energy helps you to tap into what you are feeling at any given moment - ask, and it will reply. Your heart energy allows you to show care, empathy and compassion for others, and also for yourself. It is an essential energy for forming relationships and partnerships. Too much can cause you to disregard your mind energy and lose sight of the facts, so called 'heart over head' mentality.

Soul Energy: This is the energy associated with purpose, passion and creativity. This energy helps you tap into what it is that you want for yourself - your 'why', your reason for being. It is the energy associated with being alive, with being a living, breathing soul on this planet. When your soul energy is aligned with your strengths, you are 'in flow'. Anything feels possible, time passes and things happen without you being consciously aware. Your strengths are indications of your calling. By identifying them and putting them to work, you can discover a never-ending supply of soul energy.

Based on the work of Steve Radcliffe, Leadership Plain and Simple, 2010.

- Which of the four energies resonate most?
- Which feel naturally stronger for you?
- Which feel less strong?
- How do each of these energies manifest for you personally? You might like to associate your own words with each - go with your gut; there's no right or wrong answer.
- What do you do to recharge each energy? For example, if your body energy is particularly important to you, but your job requires you to sit for long periods, what do you do to recharge your body energy during your breaks or before or after work?

When you manage your energies well you vibrate differently. You tune in to the natural vibration of the universe and begin to work with, rather than against yourself.

ADJUST YOUR KNOBS

Managing your energies allows you to get shit done without exhausting yourself, especially if you have a lot on your plate and you feel like you are juggling priorities. Think of your priorities as a set of dials or knobs. You can have any number of them, although be warned that the number of knobs you have on the go at any one time will contribute towards feelings of stress, strain, overwhelm and burnout, even if they are all set to 'low'. You can only spin plates for so long before you end up dropping one.

You might have knobs for any of the following, plus anything that feels particularly important to you in your life right now.

Family, Kids, Partner, Pets, Work, Self-Care, Exercise, Hobbies, Relationships, Friends, Projects, etc.

Are your knobs set correctly?

- What knobs do you have? Try labelling them.
- How much of your time and energy are you giving to each? You can set your knobs from

1-10, low, medium, high or red, amber, green. Whichever works for you.

- How satisfied are you with the positioning of your knobs?
- Which knobs require some adjustment? Just a small tweak here and there can make a big difference.

The aim here isn't to distribute your time and energy equally amongst each of them. Try as you may, dear Diva, there is only one of you and you can only spread yourself so thinly before it begins to show. Instead, make some decisions about what feels more or less important to you right now. You can readjust them at any time you like as priorities come and go and as the seasons change. For example, in the summer, you might dial up hobbies and dial down self-care because you are spending more time outside in the fresh air and the sunshine and your hobbies replenish you. In the winter, you may wish to dial up relationships and self-care to account for the winter weather and dark nights; anything goes. Your knobs will always be set differently to those of the people around you. Avoid comparing how you spend your time with how others spend theirs; we are each just doing our best to get by. Lastly, don't forget that you aren't supposed to be going at it alone. Use the people around you to help keep you focused on your priorities. Your entourage really is the best resource you have at your disposal - use them.

YOUR ISLAND OF SANITY

Of course, one way to avoid stress and burnout is to take regular holidays. Wouldn't it be lovely to be able to fly away to your very own tropical island whenever things started to feel tough so that you could rest, recharge and return with a new-found sense of perspective and focus? I mean, should you be a member of the billionaire elite then you may well be able to. Chances are, you don't have that luxury. However, you can still experience some of the benefits in the very seat you're sitting in now. How? By creating your very own Island of Sanity. I've retreated to my Island of Sanity frequently over the years and have encouraged people I've worked with to cultivate their own. There are no rules when it comes to creating yours. My gift to you is a blank cheque and as many resources as you need to create a place that rejuvenates your mind, body, heart and soul. Your island can be any size or shape. It can be just off the coast or in the middle of nowhere. It can be populated or you can be completely alone.

Your Island of Sanity is a place you can visit when you start to feel anxious, worried or stressed and you just need five minutes to centre yourself, to gather your thoughts and emotions before stepping back onto the mainland and doing your thing.

Consider what your own island would be like. Visit it when required and experience its grounding and healing properties. Here's how it goes:

TAKING CARE OF YOURSELF

You've arrived on your very own Island of Sanity.

- Where is it? Is it just off the coast so that you can people watch from a distance, or is it the middle of nowhere?
- What does it look like? Is it big or small?
- What's the climate like? Is it a lush green forest? A desert island? A tropical island of tall palms and endless sandy beaches? Or something else?
- Where do you stay when you're there? 7-star hotel or a shack on the beach?
- Is there anybody there with you? Your family or best friends? Butlers in the buff? Or are you completely alone?
- How do you spend your time when you're there? Do you walk? Rest? Get a massage? Read? Or do you do something fun, thrilling and exhilarating?
- What do you not do when you're there?
- Is there music? Or do you prefer to listen to the sound of the waves and the wildlife?
- What do you like to eat there? Do you find it and cook it yourself? Or do you have a team of Michelin-starred chefs at your beck and call?
- Most importantly, what do you wear? Do you prefer the t-shirt and shorts look? Or are you more Joan Collins?
- Lastly, if you were to name your island, what would you call it?

Make a point of visiting, if only for a few minutes and really feel what it's like to be there.

Your Island of Sanity is a particularly good place to go if you find yourself caught up in the heat of the moment and you can't easily get outside to experience the healing properties of nature. If you find yourself in this position, then give this a go:

- Close your eyes.
- Turn your attention to your breathing. Take a few big breaths in and out through your nose.
- When you've steadied yourself and you feel ready, step ashore your island of sanity.
- Now fully immerse yourself in your island experience. Take note of:

  » 5 things that you can see around you.
  » 4 things that you can touch.
  » 3 things that you can hear.
  » 2 things that you can smell.
  » 1 thing that you can taste.

Here's an example from my own Island of Sanity.

- I can see: A run-down beach shack made of driftwood with light-blue painted shutters that have faded in the sun, fish swimming in the crystal-clear waters, the leaves of palm trees blowing in the gentle breeze, my own bare footprints in the sand behind me and tropical birds flying high above.

- I can touch: The warm sand between my toes, the rough fibrous trunk of a palm tree, the smooth and shiny leaves of a nearby plant and the ridges of a shell washed up on the beach.
- I can hear: The calls of parrots in the faraway trees, the creaks of the palm trees gently swaying the breeze and the shuffling sound of the sand beneath my feet.
- I can smell: The sweet scent of tropical flowers drifting on the breeze and the smell of an approaching rainstorm that's needed to clear the air and nourish the flora.
- I can taste: The salty spray of the waves crashing onto the rocks.

SLEEP TIGHT, SHINE BRIGHT LIKE A DIVA

A diva needs their beauty sleep. If, like me, you aren't much of a morning person, then getting enough sleep becomes even more important in making sure that you can deal with hours between 07:00 and noon without getting into trouble. It's easy to get in a tizz when you're running on near empty. The health benefits of getting enough, good-quality sleep are well-researched. I won't attempt to recount them. However, I will share some top tips for increasing your chances of getting a good night's sleep so that you can sleep tight and shine bright. Give them a go but as always, take what you want and leave what you don't; find a routine that works for you.

Before bed:

- Set an 'anti-alarm' an hour or so before you want to go to bed. During this time, avoid using technology or anything that is going to over-stimulate you. This is wind-down time.
- Limit distractions. Try putting your phone on 'Do Not Disturb' a couple of hours before bed. Mine comes on automatically at 21:00 every evening.
- If you can, keep to a routine and go to bed at around the same time each evening. Your brain will soon pick up on it and start sending messages to your body to prepare you for sleep when it knows the time is coming.
- Do all the obvious stuff like making sure the room is dark, is as cool or as warm as you like it and that it feels like a restful space. If there's stuff everywhere and you have to clear the bed before you get into it, then by the time you've done it you'll be stimulated and less primed for sleep.
- If you like silence, great. If you'd rather be rocked to sleep by the sounds of nature or white noise, then make use of your smart speaker. You can ask it to play all sorts, anything from thunderstorms and ocean waves to whale song.

Sleep is the best meditation - Dalai Lama

BEDTIME YOGA

If you struggle to get to sleep because either your mind is whirring or you get fidgety legs, then give yoga a go. If yoga isn't your thing, then look at it as stretching; it's the same. There are some really easy bedtime yoga stretches that can be done on your bed, in your pj's! They are gentle poses that help to relax your body and your mind, relieving stress and tension in your muscles and helping to quieten an over-active mind. Google 'bedtime yoga' and then go to images; you're bound to find something that works for you.

WAKE UP LIKE A DIVA

How you start your day matters. If you wake up in a bad mood, you're rushing around, skip breakfast and stomp to the car, the chances are you aren't going to be spreading much love that morning. In fact, it's more likely that people will be doing their best to keep clear of you. If unchecked, your mood can easily spiral and before you know it, you're acting independently of yourself. You might find yourself being short with somebody or behaving in a way that is out of character, whilst a little voice at the back of your head is shouting, *No, don't do it!* But you just can't help yourself. You're running on autopilot, on a collision course, but you can't quite bring yourself to pull the breaks. Bad moods can quickly develop momentum, especially if you start looking for even more reasons to be annoyed. For example, Julie didn't acknowledge you when you walked into the office, even though you have a face that looked like a bulldog chewing a bee - it must mean she's being funny with you. You go to make a drink but there's no milk left - the selfish lot have drunk it all and left none for you - they probably had a right good laugh about it at your expense (the milk ran out yesterday by the way and so nobody had any this morning).

When you're caught up in a snowball that's rolling down a mountain at 100 miles an hour, it doesn't take long before you have an avalanche on your hands - we've all been there at some point. How does it end? Well, if you aren't able to pull yourself out of it (See Triggers and Switches in the chapter titled 'Knowing Yourself'), then the best you can hope for is to make it out alive and to write the day off and try again tomorrow.

Of course, you will have days like that from time to time; you're only human and there's only so much you can take before you switch into survival mode and focus on just getting by. Having a good morning routine can set you off on the right path, even if you wake up a bit grumpy. Starting your day gently and deliberately, by that I mean choosing your mood and your actions, rather than running on autopilot, will increase your chances of having a more grounded and productive day. Things will come easier, and what's even better? Your positive energy will mean that people will enjoy being around you.

Rather than wake up to an alarm that sounds like a submarine being torpedoed, choose a song or a piece of music that will make you smile before you've even opened your eyes. I'll let you into a secret, my morning wake-up is the sound of an audience cheering and clapping. R.J Palacio once said:

I think there should be a rule that everybody should get a standing ovation at least once in their lives.

Well, I get mine every morning. It's fun, it's ridiculous and it means I've got my first laugh of the day in by 07:10!

Rather than jumping straight out of bed, give yourself a few minutes to just lay there. Sit with your thoughts for a while. Avoid any inclination to pick up your phone. Just 'be' for a moment. How did you sleep? What did you dream about? How does your body feel? How do you want your day to go?

Setting an intention for the day sends a clear message to all the different parts of you - your body, mind and spirit, about the day ahead. This is less about *what* you want to do, and more about *how* you want to be.

For example:

- Today, I am going to slow down, cut myself some slack and take more notice of what's going on around me.
- Today, I am going to stand up for myself and say no to people who try and take me for a fool.
- Today, I will spread love, kindness and joy.
- Today, I am going to behave like a true diva. Watch out world, I'm coming for you!

Doing some light stretching in the morning can wake up your tight body, get rid of muscle stiffness and help to let go of any remaining stress from the day before. Focusing on your breathing whilst stretching ensures that your brain gets plenty of fresh oxygen, boosting your focus and concentration for the day. There are so many great morning stretch routines available online. Just Google 'morning stretches' and go to images - then give a few a go and see which you prefer. Just know that if you haven't done something like this before, it's unlikely to feel natural to start with. You will be thinking about what to do next, you will be conscious of which breath you're 'supposed' to be taking - in or out and it may even feel like hard work. Just keep going and in a few weeks, you will see what I mean. Any movement is better than no movement at all. Be patient with yourself.

AFFIRM, BITCH.

What are affirmations all about? They are positive things that you say to yourself, about yourself. They can be totally random and you can say whatever comes into your mind that morning or you can create one that you begin each day by saying. Affirmations are designed to boost your mood and your confidence, ease any anxiety and send you off into the world ready to do your thing. There's no right or wrong way. You can write your affirmation down, you can close your eyes and meditate on it or you can say it aloud in the mirror whilst putting on your war paint - that's how I like to do it. I look myself in the eye and say it like I really mean it. There are endless examples that you can find online; take a look and see which resonate.

An affirmation opens the door. It is a beginning point on the path to change - Louise Hay

DIVA JUICE (I KNOW, I'M SORRY)

If you're looking for a perky little pick-me-up to boost your mood and your energy in the morning, then poor yourself a glass of ice-cold Diva Juice...You know, there was a time when I thought I was going to be a serious author. This is so much more fun!

Green juices require hardly any digestion, so all that goodness gets to work in your body straight away. Nourishing you, dear Diva, from the inside out.

Here are just a few benefits that come from drinking green juices:

- Improved focus and mental clarity.
- Weight regulation.
- Improved bone and joint function.
- Stronger immune system.
- Healthier hair, skin and nails.
- More energy!

This juice is one that I swear by, particularly in the winter when it takes a bit more oomph to get the engine going. A glass of Diva Juice first thing, ideally 20 minutes before or after any other food or drink, will have you leaving the house feeling energised and inspired to put your best pedicured foot forward.

In truth, you could make this using any green vegetables and citrus fruit you like.

Here's how I make mine:

- As much frozen spinach as you can fit in your blender.
- And then any other green veg that you have in the fridge or freezer: broccoli, asparagus, kale, celery, etc.
- A peeled orange (you can add apple/lime too if you like).
- If you want a kick, add as much raw ginger as you like.
- Then add water and blitz to the thickness you prefer.

Bottoms/tits up!

—CHAPTER SEVENTEEN—

SPIRITUALITY

A diva knows that there is no 'me and them', only 'us'.

ONENESS

You probably didn't expect to find a chapter about spirituality in a book about being a diva. I ummed and ahhed about whether to include it - in the end, I decided to offer you the choice, dear Diva, as to whether you read it or not - after all, that's your prerogative.

The world of the diva and the world of spirituality intersect with the idea of oneness. This is the idea that everything and everyone in the universe is connected. This includes every living being and every aspect of the natural world. In previous chapters, we've explored the idea that a diva is neither above nor below any other living being. That we are all created equal and that we are all here with the same aim - to get by. With that in mind and with the knowledge that our time on Earth is finite, we have the choice of two paths. We can take the path that leads to a life of:

- Telling ourselves we aren't good or worthy enough.
- Self-doubt and not believing in ourselves.
- Being afraid of failure (and of success).
- Worrying about things which we can't control.
- Unrealised dreams and goals.
- Frustration, regret and 'what ifs?'

Or we can take another path - the path of the diva. For this reason, oneness had to feature. And if you only read one part of this chapter, make it this one.

Oneness is often linked to spirituality, with most religions believing in the interconnectedness of all things. One of the key aspects of oneness is the idea that everything is made up of universal energy. This energy is constantly flowing and moving, connecting everything in the universe. Meaning that all living beings are connected and it's this connection which allows us to feel empathy and compassion for one another.

Oneness also teaches that there is no separation between the 'self' and the outer world. This is why pre-supposing success and 'blagging it 'til we bag it' is so effective because it means that our actions and thoughts have an impact not only on ourselves but also on the world around us - on our reality. See 'Law of Attraction' in the chapter titled 'Blag It 'til You Bag It'.

Beyond spirituality, oneness has practical applications in our daily lives. By recognising our interconnectedness with the world, we can develop a greater sense of empathy and compassion for others. We can also become more aware of how our actions impact the environment, and we can take steps to reduce our environmental impact. Our interconnectedness with the universe can help us to develop a greater sense of purpose and meaning in our lives, by waking up and seeing life for what it really is, the moment by moment process of...well, living. Of taking care of ourselves and the people we love. Of being kind to ourselves, to others and to the world around us. It's not the 'rat race' or chasing the biggest salaries or the fanciest houses or cars, but rather just being in the moment and living life to its fullest.

Oneness is powerful. It can transform the way we view ourselves and the world around us. By recognising our interconnectedness with others and the environment, we can develop greater empathy, compassion and a clearer sense of purpose in our lives. Oneness has the potential to bring about positive change in us and in doing so, in the world - and lord knows the world needs it.

Take notice of the world around you, dear Diva. Whatever you lay your eyes on is made up of the same universal energy as you. When you harm yourself, you harm the world. When you take steps to heal the world, you heal yourself.

One of the best-kept secrets in this world is that we are all uniquely different and yet gloriously the same. The ego perceives us as separate from one another, but we aren't. We are the same thing.

WHAT'S IT ALL ABOUT?

Spirituality helps you connect with something greater than yourself. Whether you believe in God, the universe, or Mother Nature, having a connection to something bigger than yourself can give you a sense of purpose and meaning that you just can't get from material possessions, however gorgeous they are. Spirituality also helps you to find inner calm. In a world that's constantly bombarding us with stress and chaos, taking the time to meditate or simply stop, notice and reflect, can do wonders for your mental health. It can help to reduce anxiety, improve your mood and even boost your immune system.

But that's not all. Spirituality can also help you develop greater compassion and empathy for others. When you start to see the interconnectedness of all things, it becomes easier to treat others with kindness and understanding. And let's be real, the world could use a lot more of that right about now.

I've been searching for ways to heal myself, and I've found that kindness is the best way.
- Lady Gaga

And last but not least, spirituality can help you find your own truth and purpose. By exploring your spiritual beliefs and values, you can get a better sense of who you are and what you want out of life. It can help you align your actions with the things that you stand for (your values) and make decisions that are in line with your highest self.

We are each a manifestation of stardust. Spiritual beings having a human experience for a brief moment in time. It's my belief that when our brief 'flash in the pan' is over, we'll be able to look back on our time on this rock and think about what we learned. Not in the form of some judgement leading to either the pearly gates or the fiery pits, but in the form of a sort of 'life review'. Perhaps a bit like a West-End review in the Sunday Times, except at the end of your 'run', you get to write the review yourself. With the advantage of distance and the loss of ego from your human form, we get to look back on how we spent our time - the things we did or didn't do. The times when we were kind. The times when we weren't - and everything in between. When the paper hits the celestial doormat, how would you like your review to read? Buy into that idea as much or as little as you please.

If religion is a collective experience, the coming together of people to worship, then spirituality is said to be an individual practice. What's it all about? I have a few thoughts, see which resonate with you. The point is it's individual. If you have a definition for what spirituality means to you, it will be yours - that's the point.

- Perspective: There's always more going on than meets the senses.
- Inclusion: We are all the same and we are deeply connected.
- Formless: It has no sacred space or symbol; it's all around us.
- Experience: It's about individual experience rather than belief.
- Individual: It's something different for everybody. It's practised differently and yet still 100% correct.
- Self: Experiencing a connection to your 'higher self' - your spiritual self. The self without form or ego.
- More: There's more to life than mere existence and that which we observe in physical form.
- Practice: It's an individual recipe of thoughts and actions that increase our connection to each other and to something beyond our senses.
- Present: It deals with the only thing we ever have - the present moment. This human experience is the thing to focus on, not what happens afterwards or where we go or don't go when it's over.
- Suffering: An understanding that suffering is part of the human experience. Through it, we gain a deeper understanding of ourselves, of the world around us, of our place and of the present moment.

- Some*thing*: A belief in some*thing* greater, rather than some*one*.
- Meaning: A search for either our individual purpose, *What am I here to do?* Or for meaning in life itself, *Why am I here?*

What would you add or remove from this list?

We are not human beings having a spiritual experience. We are spiritual beings having a human experience - Pierre Teilhard de Chardin

SIGNS OF SPIRITUALITY

You might have a clear sense as to whether you consider yourself a spiritual person or not. If you aren't sure, then here are a few signs that I've picked up over the years. See if any of them resonate:

- Having/searching for a higher sense of purpose.
- Having/searching for the meaning in life.
- Having a greater sense of self-esteem and self-control.
- Being able to regulate your emotions.
- Having a positive relationship with yourself.
- Having a greater level of empathy and intuition, knowing what's going on for somebody without them having to say.
- Understanding that multiple truths can exist.

- Having a sense of perspective. We see things not as they are, but as *how* we are.
- Believing that life is to be embraced.
- Being curious about life after death.
- Feeling connected to something greater than yourself.
- Speaking aloud to the universe. *I see what you did there, thanks!*
- Noticing 'signs' - a white feather, a robin etc.
- Being hopeful when things get tough.
- 'Being' in the present moment; practicing mindfulness.
- Practicing meditation, breathing practices or yoga.

FINDING YOUR FLOW

There are few greater feelings than that of being in flow. This is a state you experience when you are totally immersed in what you are doing, beyond the point of distraction. You've heard the phrase 'in the zone'? Well flow is that and then some. Being in flow means actually enjoying what you are doing beyond mere concentration. Concentration is something you attempt to 'do'; meanwhile flow is something that happens to you. Your mind quietens, your focus narrows and you experience life in a way that transcends time. Before you know it, hours have passed, people around you have come and gone, noise and conversation have been placed on mute - life itself has had its pause button pressed. Meanwhile, totally unaware of your surroundings, you've been conjuring up your very own form of magic. You stop, look at the fruits of your labour and think, *Jeez, where did that come from?* The flow state can be accessed by anybody. All it takes is to identify those things that you are good at *and* that give you energy (your strengths) and then put them to work. By that, I mean finding a way that you can use your strengths in an activity that brings you joy, purpose and meaning. For me, flow comes when I'm channelling my creativity, when I'm writing, painting or designing. Channelling is actually the right word to use in this instance because it feels just like that. When I'm in flow, I immediately know the next steps to take. It's almost like someone is on my shoulder, whispering instructions into my ear. It's a peaceful place, it's quiet, it's feeling like everything is lined up just right and then something happens. I begin to let something in. Divine inspiration? I'm not sure - who knows, but at times it sure can feel that way. Whatever it is, it's nourishment for the mind, body and soul. It leaves me replenished, energised and itching to come back for more.

Find your flow. See the chapter titled 'Knowing Yourself' to find out more.

Your strengths are indications of your calling.

BREATHWORK

Congratulations, you've clearly mastered the art of breathing - OK, next! Now before you start thinking that I'm about to tell you how to breathe, don't worry, I'm not. Although, what I will say is that most of us go about our day paying very little attention to our breath. You breathe in and out about 22,000 times a day, I know, wow. Your breath is your life force; it sustains you and quite literally keeps you alive. It makes sense then that having a greater sense of connection to your breath can help you to develop a greater sense of connection to yourself and to the world around you - the very world that offers you that breath.

Nathalia Westmacott-Brown, author of 'Breathwork - Use the power of breath to energize your body and focus your mind', writes that 'Scientific research is now proving what yogis and mystics have known for years. This simple, invisible force can improve brain function, decision making, physical capabilities, endurance levels and even induce profound trans-personal meditative states'.

That way of being still with ourselves - coming back to the centre and recognising that something is more important than you - it's more important than the work you are doing, brings a kind of energy, an intention that we have never had before - Oprah Winfrey

Here are a few of my favourite breathwork practices:

Conscious Breathing: For feeling grounded and connected.

- Find a comfortable position. I like to sit in a chair with my back supported, but you could sit cross-legged or lie down. Relax your body, feel your shoulders lower and your jaw soften.
- Feel the sensation of the chair against your back or the floor beneath you. Settle into it and feel yourself being supported.
- Close your eyes and begin by noticing your breathing. How's your breathing rate? Fast or slow? Don't try to change anything at this point; just notice what you notice. This 'noticing' can tell you a lot about your current state, both physical and mental - are you relaxed/at ease? Or are you tense/anxious?
- Bring your attention to where your breath stops. Are you breathing deep into your belly? Or is your breath stopping short somewhere in your upper chest? If you aren't sure, place a hand on your tummy and notice how much it moves as you breathe in and out.
- Now begin to take deep, slow and steady breaths in and out. Try to fill your tummy with as much breath as you can. As you settle into a gentle rhythm, notice yourself feeling increasingly more relaxed and grounded.

Flush It Out: For bringing in positive, healing energy and flushing out negative, stale energy.

- Begin as above, but this time with every breath in visualise the breath entering you as a golden light, filling you up from the top of your head to your toes.
- As you breathe out, visualise any negative or stale energy leaving your body as grey smoke.
- If you are experiencing any particular physical health problems or pains, as you breathe in, send that golden breath specifically to those areas, visualise it nourishing and healing you. As you exhale, visualise the pain and stale energy leaving you.

Life's a Beach: For calming. This practice was gifted to me by my absolutely fabulous Voice Coach, Milly Ellis - Founder and CEO of BeHEARD.

- Visualise yourself sitting on the most beautiful beach with your legs out in front of you, soles facing the ocean.
- Watch the waves as they come in, the white peaks losing momentum as they move towards you, gently lapping at your feet.
- When you notice a wave that you like the look of, take a deep breath in, pulling it towards you with your breath. Keep breathing in until the wave has reached you - 5 counts.

- Hold onto the wave, feel it wash over you - 5 counts.
- As you breathe out an audible *whoosh*, send the wave back out to the ocean - 5 counts and with it, send any negativity, stress or worry.
- Repeat 5 times.

Counting: For when you are feeling stressed or anxious and you need to take a moment.

- In for 3, hold for 3, out for 3 x 3.
- In for 4, hold for 4, out for 4 x 4.
- In for 5, hold for 5, out for 5 x 5.

MEDITATION

Adding meditation to your self-care or indeed spiritual practice, can bring a sense of calm and balance to what may otherwise be a hectic day. Starting or ending your day with just 5 minutes of meditation has been proven to help reduce the impact of physical and psychological stress. It's also good for the soul. Meditating regularly keeps you grounded, focused and helps you to maintain a sense of purpose, perspective and direction.

When it comes to meditation, I hold three firm beliefs:

1. Everybody can do it, yes dear Diva, that means you too.
2. There is no right or wrong way to do it.

3. Every little helps. Just a few minutes a day can make all the difference.

There is a meditation out there for everyone. Whether you prefer a guided meditation or a more self-serve approach, whether you fancy a breath-based meditation, a mindfulness meditation, a meditation that uses repeated mantras or a visualisation meditation - they are out there at the touch of a button. You can now download some great apps that offer meditations of all types and durations. A favourite of mine is 'Insight Timer' available from the Apple App Store.

There are three meditations that I reach for to keep me doing my best diva work. They help me to stay grounded, focused and in tune with the universe, my higher self and my purpose - to be of service to others.

In meditation, I can let go of everything. I'm not Hugh Jackman. I'm not dad. I'm not a husband. I'm just dipping into that powerful source that creates everything. I take a little bath in it.
- Hugh Jackman

Breath Based: This meditation uses the Conscious Breathing exercise from above. The aim is to keep your mind as clear and free from thought as possible. Focus only on your breath and re-direct your attention back to your breath if you find your mind wanders. Pure ecstasy can be found in emptiness, but it does take practise. Be kind to yourself and gently bring yourself back to your breath each time a thought pops into your head. Some would argue that the act of noticing the thought, closing it down and re-directing yourself back to your breath, is in fact the act of meditation. What I would say, and this is a bit of a paradox, is when you have finished meditating, try and recount the things that came to you. Were there words or images that could in fact be something else? But here's another paradox, try not to over-think or draw meaning to what might well be busy brain chatter, but do stop to ask if your subconscious may just be sending you a nudge - only you will know.

Om: This meditation uses 'Om', defined in Hindu scripture as the primordial sound of creation, the original vibrational frequency of the universe, from which all other vibrations can manifest. Chanting or hearing the Om chant can calm your mind and attract positive energy to you. Begin as with the first meditation by finding a comfortable position, quieting your mind and drawing your attention to your breath. Once you've stayed there for a short while and your mind has begun to empty. Draw your attention to the sound of Om. You could chant this or, as I do, play the sound through your headphones or smart speaker. The Insight Timer app I mentioned earlier has some great Om meditations to try. Some of the most powerful meditations I've experienced have been using Om. Focus on nothing else but the sensation of the sound washing over your entire body. Give yourself over to it and allow it to nourish, heal and revitalise you.

Perspective: This is a visualisation meditation that I've developed over the years. It works with nature as a way of helping to gain a sense of perspective, particularly when things are feeling tough. It's similar to the perspective tools shared in the chapter titled 'Keeping Your Cool' and works with the same idea of zooming out on Google Earth and seeing yourself from outside of yourself. It's simple and you can spend as much time as you like visualising each element. Here's how it goes:

- Ideally, and if you are able, begin outside, seated or cross-legged. If you aren't able to be outside, open a window.
- Close your eyes, quieten your mind and bring your attention first to your body - feel the weight of your body against the chair or the ground. Feel the sensation of being supported. Then turn your attention to your breath.
- Notice your breath, but don't change it. Just breathe normally.
- When you are ready, turn your attention to the sounds and sensations around you. The sound of birds and of nature, the sensation of the breeze against your face or the grass beneath your feet.

- Now imagine that you are looking down on yourself from above, notice yourself and your surroundings from this perspective and then begin to zoom out.
- Take it a step at a time. Zoom out to your street, the cars going by, the people going about their day, then zoom out a bit more to see your town, then your city, your county, then your country, keep going until you are observing the Earth itself. Watch it as it slowly turns. When you are ready, turn your attention to the following in any order - visualise as much life as you possibly can within each...

  » Tiny streams and huge oceans.
  » Lush rainforest and dry desert.
  » Green hills and snowy mountains.

When you are ready, bring your attention back to yourself. Hover over your own head as you say aloud whatever you feel needs to be said. It could be a mantra, e.g. *I am calm, I am kind, I am loved.* Or it could be your intention for the day. Once you've said whatever needs to be said, open your eyes.

A whole new world is blown into existence at the very moment you see yourself from outside of yourself. That is wisdom.

MESSAGE TO THE UNIVERSE

Here's the thing. The universe is energy. You are made up of universal energy. Therefore, sending a message to the universe is kind of like making a request of yourself, your higher self. The version of you that exists beyond physical form, that transcends the limitations of what it means to have a human experience on this planet. It's a way of tapping into the energy that made you. And why not? What have you got to lose? When the chips are down you need all the damn help you can get.

Here's an example of a message I send when I fear that I might be losing my way, when I'm feeling out of kilter or something isn't sitting comfortably with me. It goes like this:

Universe,

I trust you to show me what you would have me do today and who you would have me speak to.

I trust you to guide me and show me what I need to know. I trust that you are leading me to solutions that are of the highest good for all.

Give it a go. Ask and see what comes back.

Everything we call real is made of things that cannot be regarded as real. If quantum mechanics hasn't profoundly shocked you, you haven't understood it - Niels Bohr (Noble Prize in Physics 1922)

TAOISM

It took me 36 years to discover Taoism, I wish I'd understood it sooner. For this reason, I'm sharing it with you - even though it is slightly paradoxical when compared with the idea of 'making' stuff happen for ourselves. As always, take what you like and leave what you don't.

Taoism is an ancient Chinese philosophy dating back to the 4th century BC that emphasises living in harmony with the 'Tao' or 'The Way'. Taoism emphasises the importance of balance and harmony in all aspects of life. Taoists believe that the universe is governed by a natural order that can be observed and followed and that by aligning ourselves with this natural order, we can achieve a state of inner and outer peace and contentment - bring it on.

One of the key concepts in Taoism is the idea of 'Wu Wei', which translates to 'non-action' or 'effortless action'. This concept teaches the importance of letting things happen naturally without forcing them - of just letting things be what they are.

Another important aspect of Taoism is the idea of 'Yin and Yang'. This is about the balance between opposing forces in the universe, such as light and shade, kindness and hatred and peace and war, etc. Taoists believe that by understanding and balancing these opposing forces, we can achieve a state of harmony and balance. Think 90's changing rooms 'Feng Shui' but without the tears at the end.

Taoism also teaches the importance of living in the present moment and letting go of attachments to the past and future. This encourages us to embrace simplicity and reject materialism, focusing instead on inner peace and contentment. By aligning ourselves with the Tao and practicing concepts such as Wu Wei and Yin and Yang, we can achieve a state of inner peace and contentment - and help others to achieve the same.

Tao gives you a feeling that you belong to the cosmos and gives purpose to your life; it gives you such a sense of identity and strength to know you're living the life you can live and therefore ought to be living. Make full use of your character and full use of your life on Earth - Vivienne Westwood

THE WAY OF THE DIVA

EPILOGUE

FINAL WORDS

Well, dear Diva, it would appear that we have come to the end of our time together. It's been a privilege to have joined you on this journey to find your inner diva. I hope that it's been a journey full of ideas, realisations, laughs and deep reflection. If it has, then I have succeeded.

It may delight you to know that this isn't, in fact, the end. Because The Way of The Diva isn't something to be read and intellectualised, but rather something to be lived. In living it, you bring it to life, not just in yourself, but in everyone you touch with your kindness, your humility and with your passion and your determination.

I ask that you do indeed live The Way of The Diva. Perhaps not all day every day, but for at least some of the day, every day. Realise deeply how important you are to this world. Go out there assured of your place within it and spread the light that shines from within you. Be the diva you are and have always been. Live unapologetically as yourself, and know that through this act of being, you inspire others to do the same.

Carry The Way of The Diva with you. When you are unsure, allow it to guide you and light your way. Ask...

What would a diva do?

And the way will be revealed.

I couldn't end without one final piece of diva wisdom. Whether it's in life, in love or in work...

Know when it's your time to go, and always leave the fans wanting more.

THE DIVA DECK

Loved The Way of The Diva and want to keep that good feeling going?...

Introducing The Diva Deck: 56 Inspiring Messages to Help You Unleash Your Inner Diva. The Diva Deck contains some of your favourite quips from the book plus many more. Each card is thoughtfully designed to elevate your self-belief, inspiring you to become a braver, bolder, and more confident you. The Diva Deck is more than just a set of cards; it's your personal cheerleader, mentor, and confidante. Whether you keep them by your bedside, tuck them in your bag, or display them proudly on your desk, The Diva Deck serves as a daily reminder of the diva within you

Visit thewayofthediva.com to get yours.

ABOUT THE AUTHOR

Adam is a writer, coach, podcast host and campaigner who has a passion for developing others and for promoting social justice. With almost two decades of experience in personal development and coaching, he is committed to empowering people, specifically women and the LGBTQ+ community, to live more fulfilling lives by embracing their inner-diva.

BAREFOOT COACHING

Adam is the Creative Director at Barefoot Coaching, a world-leading provider of professionally accredited and university-approved coach training. Having trained with Barefoot in 2020, Adam is a qualified and credentialed personal and business coach. Although his 1:1 coaching has taken a backseat in favour of his other projects and interests, Adam frequently shares the life changing transformation brought about as a result of him completing Barefoot's Postgraduate Certificate in Personal and Business Coaching. Barefoot has now trained over 5,500 coaches from all around the world, and Adam is proud to call himself a 'Barefooter'.

Adam also hosts the Barefoot Podcast, where he interviews inspirational people who are making a difference in the world through their coaching.

Search 'Barefoot Podcast' wherever you get yours.

Barefoot Coaching:
www.barefootcoaching.co.uk
Instagram / Facebook: barefootcoachingltd

FEMALE EMPOWERMENT

Adam was raised around strong women. It's this experience that instilled in him a deep sense of importance about female empowerment and women's rights. Today, he is a proud Ambassador for Broxtowe Women's Project (BWP), a small but mighty charity operating from Nottinghamshire that supports survivors of domestic abuse. BWP provide a confidential helpline, outreach service, training courses and drop-in sessions, all aimed at empowering women.

Adam is also an Ambassador for White Ribbon UK. Having made the White Ribbon Promise 'Never to use, excuse or remain silent against men's violence towards women', Adam helps to create awareness of domestic abuse related issues and promote the work of both White Ribbon UK and Broxtowe Women's Project.

Broxtowe Women's Project
www.broxtowewomensproject.org.uk
Instagram / Facebook: broxtowewomensproject

White Ribbon UK
www.whiteribbon.org.uk
Instagram / Facebook: whiteribbonuk

ANIMALS

Adam is a passionate supporter of animal welfare charities and in particular Bliss Cavalier Rescue, a charity based in the North-East of England that rescues and re-homes Cavalier King Charles Spaniels (of which he has two), the vast majority of whom arrive at the rescue with severe long-term medical conditions (as is unfortunately typical with the bread) which require expensive and life-long veterinary care.

Bliss Cavalier Rescue
www.blisscavalierrescue.org
Instagram / Facebook: blisscavalierrescue

THE LGBTQ+ COMMUNITY

As a proud gay man, Adam is an avid supporter of LGBTQ+ rights. He supports a number of local and national projects and works to promote LGBTQ+ inclusion, LGBTQ+ owned businesses and frontline LGBTQ+ services.

GIVING BACK

A proportion of the profits from the sale of The Way of The Diva will be distributed amongst Adam's chosen charities.

Should you wish to donate directly, please visit the websites of the charities mentioned. All donations are gratefully received.

CONTACT

Get in touch using the details below.

The Way of The Diva

www.thewayofthediva.com

hello@thewayofthediva.com

Instagram / Facebook: thewayofthediva

Adam Goodman-Smith

www.adamgoodmansmith.co.uk

hello@adamgoodmansmith.co.uk

Instagram / Facebook: adamgoodmansmith

Media Enquiries:

kathryn@edenpr.co.uk / enquiries@edenpr.co.uk

0115 958 8850